STYLISTICS

In ...*ics* Richard Bradford provides a definitive introductory g... o modern critical ideas on literary style and stylistics. The book includes examples of poems, plays and novels from Shakespeare to the present day.

This comprehensive and accessible guidebook for undergraduates explains the terminology of literary form, considers the role of stylistics in twentieth-century criticism, and shows, with worked examples, how literary style has evolved since the sixteenth century.

This book falls into three sections: Part I follows the discipline of stylistics from classical rhetoric to poststructuralism; Part II looks at the relationship between literary style and its historical context; Part III considers the relationships between style and gender, and between style and evaluative judgement.

Richard Bradford is Professor of English at the University of Ulster. He has written books on Kingsley Amis, Roman Jakobson, Milton, eighteenth-century criticism, visual poetry and linguistics.

THE NEW CRITICAL IDIOM

Series Editor: John Drakakis, University of Stirling

The New Critical Idiom is an invaluable series of introductory guides to today's critical terminology. Each book:

- provides a handy, explanatory guide to the use (and abuse) of the term

- offers an original and distinctive overview by a leading literary and cultural critic

- relates the term to the larger field of cultural representation.

With a strong emphasis on clarity, lively debate and the widest possible breadth of examples, *The New Critical Idiom* is an indispensable approach to key topics in literary studies.

- See below for new books in this series.

STYLISTICS

Richard Bradford

LONDON AND NEW YORK

First published 1997
by Routledge
11 New Fetter Lane, London EC4P 4EE

Simultaneously published in the USA and Canada
by Routledge
29 West 35th Street, New York, NY 10001

© 1997 Richard Bradford

Typeset in Adobe Garamond and Scala Sans by
Keystroke, Jacaranda Lodge, Wolverhampton

Printed and bound in Great Britain by
Clays Ltd., St Ives PLC

British Library Cataloguing in Publication Data
A catalogue record for this book is available from the British Library

Library of Congress Cataloging in Publication Data
Bradford, Richard
        Stylistics / Richard Bradford.
             p. cm. – (The new critical idiom)
        Includes bibliographical references and index.
        1. Style, Literary. I. Title. II. Series.
    PN203.B68 1997
    809–dc20   96–27990
                                                       CIP

ISBN 0–415–09768–1
      0–415–09769–X(pbk)

To Jennifer Ford

Contents

Acknowledgements

I am grateful to the Faculty of Humanities and the School of English, University of Ulster, for providing me with the time to finish this book, and to John Drakakis, a scrupulous editor.

The author and publisher are grateful for the permission to reproduce extracts from T.S. Eliot, *Collected Poems 1909–1962*, reprinted courtesy of Faber & Faber Ltd. Every effort has been made to obtain permission to use copyright material in this book. Please contact the publisher if any omissions have inadvertently occurred.

SERIES EDITOR'S PREFACE

The New Critical Idiom is a series of introductory books which seeks to extend the lexicon of literary terms, in order to address the radical changes which have taken place in the study of literature during the last decades of the twentieth century. The aim is to provide clear, well-illustrated accounts of the full range of terminology currently in use, and to evolve histories of its changing usage.

The current state of the discipline of literary studies is one where there is considerable debate concerning basic questions of terminology. This involves, among other things, the boundaries which distinguish the literary from the non-literary; the position of literature within the larger sphere of culture; the relationship between literatures of different cultures; and questions concerning the relation of literary to other cultural forms within the context of interdisciplinary studies.

It is clear that the field of literary criticism and theory is a dynamic and heterogenous one. The present need is for individual volumes on terms which combine clarity of exposition with an adventurousness of perspective and a breadth of application. Each volume will contain as part of its apparatus some indication of the direction in which the definition of particular terms is likely to move, as well as expanding the disciplinary boundaries within which some of these terms have been traditionally contained. This will involve some re-situation of terms within the larger field of cultural representation, and will introduce examples from the area of film and the modern media in addition to examples from a variety of literary texts.

INTRODUCTION

Stylistics is an elusive and slippery topic. Every contribution to the vast and multifaceted discipline of literary studies will involve an engagement with style. To accept that the subject of our attention or our critical essay is a poem, a novel or a play involves an acceptance that literature is divided into three basic stylistic registers. Even a recognition of literary studies as a separate academic sphere is prefigured by a perceived distinction between literary and non-literary texts. Stylistics might thus seem to offer itself as an easily definable activity with specific functions and objectives: stylistics enables us to identify and name the distinguishing features of literary texts, and to specify the generic and structural subdivisions of literature. But it is not as simple as this.

When we use or respond to language in the real world our understanding of what the words mean is supplemented by a vast number of contextual and situational issues: language is an enabling device; it allows us to articulate the sequence of choices, decisions, responses, acts and consequences that make up our lives. Style will play some part in this, but its function is pragmatic and purposive: we might admire the lucid confidence of the car advertisement or the political broadcast, but in the end we will look beyond the words to the potential effect of their message upon our day to day activities. The style and language of poems, novels and plays will frequently involve these purposive functions, but when we look beyond their effect to their context we face a potentially disorientating relation between what happens in the text and what might happen outside it.

Stylistics can tell us how to name the constituent parts of a literary text and enable us to document their operations, but in doing so it must draw upon the terminology and methodology of disciplines which focus upon language in the real world. The study of metre, narrative and dramatic dialogue is founded upon the fundamental units and principles of all linguistic usage: phonemes, rhythmic sequences, grammatical classes, forms of syntactic organization and so on. But these same fundamentals of communication also underpin the methodology of pure linguistics, structuralism and semiotics, discourse theory, sociolinguistics, gender studies, linguistic philosophy and a whole network of disciplines which involves the context and pragmatic purpose of communication. Consequently, modern stylistics is caught between two disciplinary imperatives. On the one hand it raises questions regarding the relation between the way that language is used and its apparent context and objective – language as an active element of the real world. On the other, it seeks to define the particular use of linguistic structures to create facsimiles, models or distortions of the real world – literary language.

This problematic relationship is the principal subject of this book. In Part I, I will consider the progress of modern stylistics from its origins in classical rhetoric to its function in modern literary studies. This will focus upon the tension between stylistics as a purely literary-critical discipline – its function in defining literature as an art form (which I call textualism) – and its operations within the broader field of structuralism and social studies (contextualism). Part II will re-examine this tension in relation to literary history: what is the relationship between literary style and historical context?

Part III is a detailed study of two issues that feature in the margins of Parts I and II. 'Gender and Evaluation' will be concerned with the way in which the twin elements of feminist criticism and women writers relate to stylistics. 'Evaluative Stylistics' will look at how the discipline of stylistics underpins our subjective experience of reading.

PART I

A SHORT HISTORY OF STYLISTICS

1

RHETORIC

The academic discipline of stylistics is a twentieth-century invention. It will be the purpose of this book to describe the aims and methods of stylistics, and we will begin by considering its relationship with its most notable predecessor – rhetoric.

The term is derived from the Greek *techne rhetorike*, the art of speech, an art concerned with the use of public speaking as a means of persuasion. The inhabitants of Homer's epics exploit and, more significantly, acknowledge the capacity of language to affect and determine non-linguistic events, but it was not until the fifth century BC that the Greek settlers of Sicily began to study, document and teach rhetoric as a practical discipline. The best-known names are Corax and Tisias who found that, in an island beset with political and judicial disagreements over land and civil rights, the art of persuasion was a useful and profitable profession. Gorgias, one of their pupils, visited Athens as ambassador and he is generally regarded as the person responsible for piloting rhetoric beyond its judicial function into the spheres of philosophy and literary studies. Isocrates was the first to extend and promote the moral and ethical benefits of the art of speech, and one of Plato's earliest Socratic dialogues bears the name *Gorgias*. It is with Plato that we encounter the most significant moment in the early history of rhetoric. In the *Phaedrus* Plato/Socrates states that unless a man pays due attention to philosophy 'he will never be able to speak properly about anything' (261A). 'A real art of speaking . . . which does not seize hold of truth, does not exist and never will' (260E). What concerned Plato was the fact that rhetoric was a device without moral or ethical subject matter. In the *Gorgias* he records an exchange between Socrates and Gorgias in which the former claims that persuasion is comparable with flattery, cooking and medicine: it meets bodily needs and satisfies physical and emotional desires. Rhetoric, he argues, is not an 'art' but a 'routine', and such a routine, if allowed to take hold of our primary communicative medium, will promote division, ambition and self-aggrandizement at the expense of collective truth and wisdom, the principal subjects of philosophy. Plato himself, particularly in the *Phaedrus*, does not go so far as to suggest the banning of rhetoric; rather he argues that it must be codified as subservient to the philosopher's search for truth.

Aristotle in his *Rhetoric* (*c.* 330 BC) produced the first counter-blast to Plato's anti-rhetoric thesis. Rhetoric, argues Aristotle, *is* an art, a necessary condition of philosophical debate. To perceive the same fact or argument dressed in different linguistic forms is not immoral or dangerous. Such a recognition – that words can qualify or unsettle a single pre-linguistic truth – is part of our intellectual training, vital to any purposive reconciliation of appearance and reality. Aristotle meets the claim that rhetoric is socially and politically dangerous with the counterclaim that the persuasive power of speech is capable of pre-empting and superseding the violent physical manifestations of subjection and defence.

The Plato–Aristotle exchange is not so much about rhetoric as an illustration of the divisive nature of rhetoric. It is replayed, with largely Aristotelian preferences, in the work of the two most prominent Roman rhetoricians, Cicero and Quintilian; it emerges in the writings of St Augustine and in Peter Ramus's *Dialectique* (1555), one of the founding moments in the revival of classical rhetoric during the European Renaissance. Most significantly, it operates as the theoretical spine which links rhetoric with modern stylistics, and stylistics in turn with those other constituents of the contemporary discipline of humanities: linguistics, structuralism and poststructuralism.

Plato and Aristotle did not disagree on what rhetoric is; their conflicts originated in the problematical relationship between language and truth. Rhetoric, particularly in Rome and in post-Renaissance education, had been taught as a form of supergrammar. It provides us with names and practical explanations of the devices by which language enables us to perform the various tasks of persuading, convincing and arguing. In an ideal world (Aristotle's thesis) these tasks will be conducive to the personal and the collective good. The rhetorician will know the truth, and his linguistic strategies will be employed as a means of disclosing the truth. In the real world (Plato's thesis) rhetoric is a weapon used to bring the listener into line with the argument which happens to satisfy the interests or personal affiliations of the speaker, neither of which will necessarily correspond with the truth. These two models of rhetorical usage are equally valid and finally irreconcilable. Lies, fabrications, exaggerations are facts of language, but they can only be cited when the fissure between language and truth is provable.

For example, if I were to tell you that I am a personal friend of Aristotle, known facts will be sufficient to convince you (unless you are a spiritualist) that I am not telling the truth. However, a statement such as, 'Aristotle speaks to me of the general usefulness of rhetoric' is acceptable because it involves the use of a familiar rhetorical device (generally termed *catachresis*, the misuse or misapplication of a term): Aristotle does not literally speak to me, but my use of the term to imply that his written words involve the sincerity or the immediate relevance of speech is sanctioned by rhetorical-stylistic convention. What I have done is to use a linguistic device to distort pre-linguistic truth and to achieve an emotive effect at the same time. My reason for doing so would be to give a supplementary persuasive edge to the specifics of my argument about the validity of Aristotle's thesis. Such devices are part of the fabric of everyday linguistic exchange and, assuming that the hearer is as conversant as the speaker with the conventions of this rhetorical game, they are not, in Plato's terms, immoral or dishonest. But for Plato such innocuous examples were merely a symptom of the much more serious consequences of rhetorical infection. The fact that Aristotle lived more than two millennia before me cannot be disputed, but the fabric of intellectual activity and its linguistic manifestation is only partly comprised of concrete facts.

Morality, the existence of God, the nature of justice: all of these correspond with the verifiable specifics of human existence, but our opinions about them cannot be verified in direct relation to these specifics. The common medium shared by the abstract and the concrete dimensions of human experience is language and, as a consequence, language functions as the battleground for the tendentious activity of making the known correspond with the unknown, that speculative element of human existence that underpins all of our beliefs about the nature of truth, justice, politics and behaviour. Plato and Aristotle named the conditions of this conflict as *dianoia* and *pragmata* (thought and facts, otherwise known as *res* or content) and *lexis* and *taxis* (word choice and arrangement, otherwise known as *verba* or form), and the distinction raises two major problems that will occupy much of our attention throughout this book.

First of all it can be argued that to make a distinction between language – in this instance the rhetorical organization of language – and the pre-linguistic continuum of thought, objects and events involves a fundamental error. Without language our experience of anything is almost exclusively internalized and private: we can, of course, make physical gestures, non-linguistic sounds or draw pictures, but these do not come close to the vast and complex network of signs and meanings shared by language users. The most important consequence of this condition of language dependency is that we can never be certain whether the private world, the set of private experiences or beliefs, that language enables us to mediate is, as Plato and Aristotle argue, entirely independent of its medium. The governing precondition for any exchange of views about the nature of existence and truth – a process perfectly illustrated by Plato's Socratic dialogues – is that language allows us to disclose the true nature of pre-linguistic fact. However, for such an exchange to take place at all each participant must submit to an impersonal system of rules and conventions. Before any disagreement regarding a fact or a principle can occur the combatants must first have agreed upon the relation between the fact/principle and its linguistic enactment. An atheist and a Christian will have totally divergent perceptions of the nature of human existence, but both will know what the word 'God' means.

The twentieth-century alternative to Aristotle's and Plato's distinction between *dianoia/pragmata* and *lexis/taxis* has been provided by Ferdinand de Saussure, a turn-of-the-century linguist whose influence upon modern ideas about language and reality has become immeasurable. Saussure's most quoted and influential propositions concern his distinction between the signified and the signifier and his pronouncement that 'in language there are only differences without positive terms'. The signifier is the concrete linguistic sign, spoken or written, and the signified is the concept represented by the sign. A third element is the referent, the pre-linguistic object or condition that stands beyond the signifier–signified relationship. This tripartite function is, to say the least, unsteady. The atheist and the Christian will share a largely identical conception of the relation between 'God' (signifier) and 'God' (signified) but the atheist will regard this as a purely linguistic state, a fiction sustained by language, but without a referent. For such an individual the signifier God relates not to a specific signified and referent, but to other signifiers and signifieds – concepts of good and bad, eternity, omniscience, omnipotence, the whole network of signs which enables Christian belief to intersect with other elements of the human condition. In Saussure's terms, the signified 'God' is sustained by the differential relationship between itself and other words and concepts, and this will override its correspondence with a 'positive term' (the referent). Plato and Aristotle shared the premise that it is dangerous and immoral to talk about something that does not exist, and that it is the duty of the philosopher to disclose such improper fissures between language and its referent. Saussure's model of language poses a threat to this ideal by raising the possibility that facts and thoughts might, to an extent, be constructs of the system of language.

The relation between classical philosophy/rhetoric and Saussurean linguistics is far more complicated than my brief comparison might suggest, but it is certain that Saussure makes explicit elements of the divisive issue of whether rhetoric is a potentially dangerous practice. And this leads us to a second problem: the relationship between language and literature. Plato in *The Republic* has much to say about literature – which at the time consisted of poetry in its dramatic or narrative forms. In Book 10 an exchange takes place regarding the nature of imitation and representation: the subject is ostensibly art, but the originary motive is as usual the determining of the nature of truth. By the end of the dialogue Socrates has established a parallel hierarchy of media and physical activities. The carpenter makes the actual bed, but the idea or concept behind this act of creation is God's. The painter is placed at the next stage down in this creative hierarchy: he can observe the carpenter making the bed and dutifully record this process. The poet, it seems, exists in a somewhat ambiguous relation to this column of originators, makers and imitators.

Perhaps they [poets] may have come across imitators and been deceived by them; they may not have remembered when they saw their works that these were but imitations thrice removed from the truth, and could easily be made without any knowledge of the truth, because they are appearances only and not realities.

(1888: 312)

In short, the poet is capable of unsettling the hierarchy which sustains the clear relation between appearance and reality. Poets, as Aristotle and Plato recognized, are pure rhetoricians: they work within a kind of metalanguage which draws continuously upon the devices of rhetoric but which is not primarily involved in the practical activities of argument and persuasion. As the above quote suggests, they move disconcertingly through the various levels of creation, imitation and deception, and as Plato made clear, such fickle mediators were not the most welcome inhabitants in a Republic founded upon a clear and unitary correspondence between appearance and reality.

Plato's designation of literature as a form which feeds upon the devices of more practical and purposive linguistic discourses, but whose function beyond a form of whimsical diversion is uncertain, has for two millenia been widely debated but has remained the dominant thesis. During the English Renaissance there was an outpouring of largely practical books on the proper use of rhetoric and rhetorical devices: for example R. Sherry's *A Treatise of Schemes and Tropes* (1550), T. Wilson's *The Arte of Rhetorique* (1553), R. Rainolde's *A Book Called the Foundacion of Rhetorike* (1563), H. Peacham's *The Garden of Eloquence* (1577) and G. Puttenham's *The Arte of English Poesie* (1589). These were aimed at users of literary and non-literary language, but a distinction was frequently made between the literary and the non-literary *function* of rhetoric. In George Puttenham's *The Arte of English Poesie* we find that there are specific regulations regarding the correspondence between literary style and subject (derived chiefly from Cicero's distinction between the grand style, the middle style and the low, plain or simple style). The crossing of recommended style–subject borders was regarded as bad writing, but a far more serious offence would be committed if the most extravagant rhetorical, and by implication literary, devices were transplanted into the serious realms of non-literary exchange. Metaphors or 'figures' are, according to Puttenham, particularly dangerous. 'For what else is your *Metaphor* but an inversion of sense by transport; your *allegorie* by a duplicitie of meaning or dissimulation under covert and darke intendments' (1589: 158). Judges, for example, forbid such extravagances because they distort the truth:

> This no doubt is true and was by then gravely considered; but in this case, because our maker or Poet is appointed not for a judge, but rather for a pleader, and that of pleasant and lovely causes and nothing perillous, such as be for the triall of life, limme, or livelihood . . . they [extravagant metaphors] are not in truth to be accompted vices but for vertues in the poetical science very commendable.

> (ibid.: 161)

Poetry does of course involve 'perillous' matters, but what Puttenham means is that the poetic function is not instrumental in activities concerned with actual 'life, limme, or livelihood'. As a spokesman for the Renaissance consensus Puttenham shows that the Plato/Aristotle debate regarding the dangers of rhetoric, especially in its literary manifestation, has been shelved rather than resolved: in short, Puttenham argues that in literature it is permissible to distort reality because literature is safely detached from the type of discourse that might have some purposive effect upon the real conditions of its participants. What Puttenham said in 1589 remains true today: literary and non-literary texts might share a number of stylistic features but literary texts do not belong in the same category of functional, purposive language as the judicial ruling or the theological tract. This begs a question which modern stylistics, far more than rhetoric, has sought to address. How do we judge the difference between literary and non-literary discourses? We have not finished with rhetoric, but in order to properly consider the two issues raised by it – the relation between language and non-linguistic reality and the difference between literary and non-literary texts – we should now begin to examine its far more slippery and eclectic modern counterpart.

2

STYLISTICS AND MODERN CRITICISM

Two groups of critics have had a major influence on the identity and direction of twentieth-century English studies: the Russian and central European Formalists and the more disparate collection of British and American teachers and writers whose academic careers began during the 1920s and 1930s. The term New Criticism is often applied to the latter group. The objectives of the majority of individuals in each group were the same: to define literature as a discourse and art form and to establish its function as something that can be properly studied. Until the late 1950s the work of these groups remained within mutually exclusive geographical and academic contexts: the New Critics in Britain and America and the Formalists in Europe. During the 1960s New Criticism and Formalism began to recognize similarities and over-laps in their goals and methods. Since the 1960s their academic predominance has been unsettled by a much broader network of interdisciplinary practices: structuralism, poststructuralism, feminism and new historicism, are all significant elements of contemporary literary studies, and each draws its methodologies and expectations from intellectual fields beyond the traditional, enclosed realms of rhetoric and aesthetics.

This, I concede, is a simplified history of twentieth-century criticism, but it provides us with a framework for an understanding of how rhetoric has been variously transformed into modern stylistics. The New Critics and the Formalists are the most obvious inheritors of the disciplines of rhetoric, in the sense that they have maintained a belief in the empirical difference between literature and other types of language and have attempted to specify this difference in terms of style and effect. Structuralism at once extended and questioned these practices by concentrating on the similarities, rather than the differences, between literature and other discourses. Poststructuralism took this a stage further by introducing the reader into the relation between literary and non-literary style, and posing the question of whether the expectations of the perceiver can determine, rather than simply disclose, stylistic effects and meanings. Feminist critics have examined style less as an enclosed characteristic of a particular text and more as a reflection of the sociocultural hierarchies – predominantly male – which control stylistic habits and methods of interpretation. Similarly, Marxists and new historicists concern themselves with style as an element of the more important agenda of cultural and ideological change and mutation.

For the sake of convenience I shall divide these different approaches to stylistics into two basic categories: textualist and contextualist. The Formalists and New Critics are mainly textualists in that they regard the stylistic features of a particular literary text as productive of an empirical unity and completeness. They do not perceive literary style as entirely exclusive to literature – rhythm is an element of all spoken language, and narrative features in ordinary conversation – but when these stylistic features are combined so as to dominate the fabric of a text, that text is regarded as literature. Contextualism involves a far more loose and disparate collection of methods. Its unifying characteristic is its concentration on the relation between text and context. Some structuralists argue that the stylistic features of poetry draw upon the same structural frameworks that enable us to distinguish between modes of dress or such social rituals as eating. Some feminists regard literary style as a means of securing attitudes and hierarchies that, in the broader context, maintain the difference between male and female roles.

The remainder of this Part is divided into three chapters. The first two will examine in basic terms how modern criticism has employed stylistics to evolve theories of poetry and fiction: these chapters will be concerned predominantly with textualist method and practice. Chapter 5 is more concerned with contextualism and will consider the ways in which the interface between text and context can unsettle textualist assumptions.

3

TEXTUALISM I: POETRY

The first part of this chapter will give brief definitions, with examples, of the devices and linguistic elements that constitute the stylistic character of post-medieval English poetry: prosody and poetic form; metre; rhyme and the stanza; the sonnet; the ode; blank verse; free verse; metaphor; syntax, diction and vocabulary. Following this is a section on critical methods, which will include examples of how the listed devices and linguistic elements are deployed by critics in their attempts to show how poetic style creates particular meanings and effects.

PROSODY AND POETIC FORM

The most basic and enduring definition of poetry is that the poem, unlike any other assembly of words, supplements the use of grammar and syntax with another system of organization: the poetic line.

The poetic line draws upon the same linguistic raw material as the sentence but deploys and uses this in a different way. Our awareness of the grammatical rules which govern the way that words are formed into larger units of meaning is based on our ability to recognize the difference between individual words. Words are made up of sound and stress, identified respectively by the phoneme and the syllable. The function of sound and stress in non-poetic language is functional and utilitarian: before we understand the operative relation between nouns, verbs, adjectives and connectives we need to be able to relate the sound and structure of a word to its meaning.

Traditional poetry uses stress and sound not only as markers and indicators of meaning but also as a way of measuring and foregrounding the principal structural characteristic of the poem: the line. In most poems written before the twentieth-century the line is constructed from a combination of two or more of the following elements:

- A specified and predictable number of syllables. The most commonly used example of this is the ten-syllable line, the pentameter.

- A metrical pattern consisting of the relation between the stress or emphasis of adjacent syllables. The most frequently used metrical pattern in English involves the use of the iambic foot, where an emphatic syllable follows a less emphatic one, with occasional variations, or 'stress reversals'.

- Rhyme. The repetition of the phonemic sound of a single syllable at the end of a line.

- Assonance and alliteration. The repetition of clusters of similar vowel or consonant sounds within individual lines and across sequences of lines.

The persistent and predictable deployment of two or more of these features is what allows us to recognize the traditional line as an organizing feature of most pre-twentieth-century poems.

METRE

The iambic pentameter, consisting of ten syllables with the even syllables stressed more emphatically than the odd, is the most frequently used line in English poetry. It is the governing principle of Shakespeare's blank verse; of non-dramatic blank verse poems, including John Milton's *Paradise Lost* (1667) and William Wordsworth's *Prelude*; and of the heroic couplet, the structural centrepiece of most of the poems of John Dryden and Alexander Pope. Examples of its shorter version, the octosyllabic line or tetrameter can be found in many of the couplet poems of Swift, in Matthew Arnold's 'Stanzas from the Grand Chartreuse' (1885), and in Alfred, Lord Tennyson's *In Memoriam* (1850). The iambic pentameter consists of five iambic feet, its tetrameter counterpart of four. The following are examples of these, with ´ indicating the most emphatic and - the less emphatic syllables.

IAMBIC PENTAMETER: Súch pl͞eas | ur͞e tóok | t͞he Sérp | ent tó | be͞hold
(from Milton's *Paradise Lost*)

IAMBIC TETRAMETER: T͞wo cóll | ͞ege Sóphs | o͞f Camb | r͞idge gŕowth
(from Swift's 'Cassinus and Peter')

These are examples of stress-syllabic metre, in which a consistent balance is maintained between the number of syllables of a line and its stress pattern. Alternative stress-syllabic lines include seven-syllable tetrameters (see William Blake's 'The Tyger'), which are comprised of three iambic feet and a single stressed syllable,

Tý | ge͞r Tý | ge͞r, búr | n͞ing b͟right.

Lines such as this, with an odd number of syllables, can also be scanned as trochaic

(/–): Týge͞r | Týge͞r | búrni͞ng | b͟right.

The trochaic foot more frequently features as a substitute or

variation in a line of iambic feet. This occurs in the first foot
of Shakespeare's line:

Nów is | the win | tēr óf | oūr dis | cōntént.

Stress-syllabic lines consisting of three-syllable feet are generally
associated with comic poetry and song. The three-syllable foot
creates a rhythmic pattern that deviates from the modulation of
ordinary speech far more than its two-syllable counterpart; as in
Oliver Goldsmith's couplet, consisting of anapestic (– – /)feet.

Heře lies | Dāvid Gár | rick, dēscríbe | him who cán
Añ abridge | mēnt ōf all | that is pléas | ant iñ mán.

Some poems vary the syllabic length of a line, while maintaining
the same number of emphatic or stressed syllables in each. This is
called pure stress metre. An early example of pure stress metre is
Samuel Taylor Coleridge's 'Christabel' (1816) and a more recent
one occurs in T. S. Eliot's 'Ash Wednesday' (1930), in which the
differing length of each line is anchored to a repeated pattern of
two major stresses.

Lády of silences
Cálm and distréssed
Tórn and most whole
Róse of mémory

The internal structure of the poetic line is only one element of its
function as the organizing principle of poetry.

RHYME AND THE STANZA

Rhyme binds lines together into larger structural units. The
smallest of these is the couplet, rhyming aa bb cc (as in the majority
of poems by Dryden, Pope and Jonathan Swift). More complex
rhyme schemes enable the poet to create stanzas, the simplest of
these being the quatrain, rhyming ab ab. (The octosyllabic quatrain

is used by John Donne in 'The Ecstasy' and its pentameter counterpart in Thomas Gray's 'Elegy Written in a Country Churchyard'
(1751).)

The stanza can play a number of roles in the broader structure
of the poem. Narrative poems, which tell a story, often use the
stanza as a way of emphasizing a particular event or observation
while tying this into the broader narrative (as in Edmund
Spenser's long *The Faerie Queene*, John Keats's *The Eve of St Agnes*
and Lord Byron's *Don Juan*). Tennyson's *In Memoriam* uses the so-
called 'envelope stanza' (a b b a). This couplet within a couplet
provides a formal counterpoint to the tragic or emotional focus of
each stanza.

Shorter, lyric poems which focus on a specific sensation, feeling
or single event often use the stanza as a counterpoint to improvisation and spontaneity. Donne's 'The Relic' consists of three very
complicated stanzas.

8 syllables	When my grave is broke up again
8 syllables	Some second guest to entertain,
8 syllables	(For graves have learned that woman-head
8 syllables	To be to more than one a bed)
6 syllables	And he that digs it spies
10 syllables	A bracelet of bright hair about the bone,
7 syllables	Will he not let us alone
10 syllables	And think that there a loving couple lies,
10 syllables	Who thought that this device might be some way
10 syllables	To make their souls, at the last busy day
10 syllables	Meet at this grave, and make a little stay?

On the one hand the complex permutations of line length and
rhyme scheme create the impression of flexibility and improvisation, as if the metrical structure of the poem is responding to and
following the varied emphases of speech. But this stanzaic structure is repeated, with admirable precision, three times; and as
we read the poem in its entirety we find that the flexibility of the
syntax is matched by the insistent inflexibility of the stanza.

THE SONNET

The sonnet resembles the stanza in that it consists of an integrated unit of metre and rhyme: the Shakespearian sonnet consisting of three iambic pentameter quatrains followed by an iambic pentameter couplet, its Petrarchan counterpart rhyming abba abba cdc dcd. It differs from the stanza in that the sonnet is a complete poem. Most sonnets will emphasize a particular event or theme and tie this into the symmetries, repetitions and parallels of its metrical and rhyming structure.

THE ODE

The most flexible and variable stanzaic form will be found in the ode. Wordsworth's 'Ode on Intimations of Immortality' consists of eleven sections. Each of these has a pattern of metre and rhyme just as complex and varied as Donne's stanza in 'The Relic', except that in the 'Immortality Ode' the same pattern is never repeated. The open, flexible structure of the ode is well suited to its use, especially by the Romantic poets, as a medium for personal reflection; it rarely tells a particular story, and it eschews logical and systematic argument in favour of an apparently random sequence of questions, hypotheses and comparisons.

BLANK VERSE

A form which offers a similar degree of freedom from formal regularity is blank verse, consisting of unrhymed iambic pentameters. Prior to Milton's *Paradise Lost* blank verse was regarded as a mixture of poetry and prose. It was thought appropriate only for drama, in which language could be recognizably poetic (i.e. metrical) while maintaining realistic elements of dialogue and ordinary speech (without rhyme). *Paradise Lost* offered blank verse as an alternative to the use of the stanza or the couplet in longer narrative or descriptive poems.

Milton's blank verse creates a subtle tension between the iambic pattern of each line and the broader flow across lines of descriptive or impassioned speech (see below, pp. 28–9, for an example). A similar balance between discursive or reflective language and the metrical undertow of the blank verse line is found in the eighteenth-century tradition of landscape poems (see James Thomson's *The Seasons* and William Cowper's *The Task*) and in Wordsworth's 'Tintern Abbey' and *The Prelude*. The most flexible examples of blank verse, where it becomes difficult to distinguish between prose rhythm and metre, are found in the poems of Robert Browning, particularly *The Ring and the Book* (1868–9):

> So
> Did I stand question and make answer, still
> With the same result of smiling disbelief,
> Polite impossibility of faith.

FREE VERSE

Before the twentieth-century, poems which involved neither rhyme nor the metrical pattern of blank verse were rare. Christopher Smart's *Jubilate Agno* (1756) and Walt Whitman's *Leaves of Grass* (1855) replaced traditional metre with patterns redolent of biblical phrasing and intonation, and Blake in his later visionary poems (1789–1815) devised a very individual form of free verse. It was not until this century that free verse became an established part of the formal repertoire of English poetry.

Free verse (from the French *vers libre*) is only free in the sense that it does not conform to traditional patterns of metre and rhyme. The poetic line is maintained as a structural counterpoint to syntax, but is not definable in abstract metrical terms.

Free verse can be divided into three basic categories:

1. Poetry which continues and extends the least restrictive elements of traditional poetry, particularly those of the ode

and blank verse. T. S. Eliot's 'The Love Song of J. Alfred Prufrock' (1917) is a monologue with an unpredictable rhyme scheme and a rhythmic structure that invokes traditional metre but refuses to maintain a regular beat or pattern. A similar effect is achieved in W. H. Auden's 'Musée des Beaux Arts'. In *The Four Quartets* (1935–42) Eliot often uses an unrhymed form that resembles blank verse, of which the following, from the beginning of 'Little Gidding', is an example:

Mídwinter spríng is its own séason
Sémpitérnal though sódden towárds súndown,
Suspénded in tíme, betwéen póle and trópic.

The lines of the poem vary between 9 and 13 syllables. Regular metre is replaced by the distribution of three to five major stresses across each line. Although the lines cannot be scanned according to expectations of regularity they do create the impression that Eliot is giving special attention to rhythmic structure.

2. Poems in which the line structure reflects the apparent spontaneity of ordinary speech, where, unlike in 'Little Gidding', no concessions are made to a metrical undertow. Line divisions will often be used as an imitation of the process through which we transform thoughts, impressions and experiences into language. Easthope (1983) calls this form 'intonational metre'. A typical example of this is D. H. Lawrence's 'Snake'.

A snake came to my water-trough
On a hot, hot day, and I in pyjamas for the heat,
To drink there.

3. Poems in which the unmetrical line variously obstructs, deviates from or interferes with the movement of syntax.

In Ezra Pound's 'In a Station of the Metro' the two lines function as an alternative to the continuities of grammar.

The apparition of those faces in the crowd
Petals on a wet black bough.

The space between the lines could be filled by a variety of imagined connecting phrases: 'are like', 'are unlike', 'remind me of', 'are as lonely as'. Individual lines offer specific images or impressions: the reader makes connections between them.

In William Carlos Williams's 'Spring and All' the line structure orchestrates the syntax and creates a complex network of hesitations and progressions, and for an example of this turn to pp. 154–7.

The most extreme example of how the free verse line can appropriate and disrupt the structural functions of syntax will be found in the poems of e. e. cummings, where the linear movement of language is effectively broken down into visual units.

The best, brief guide to the mechanics of prosody and metre is Hobsbaum's *Metre, Rhythm and Verse Form* (1996). A more methodical survey of linguistics and poetic form is Bradford's *A Linguistic History of English Poetry* (1993). T. V. F. Brogan's *English Versification 1570–1980* (1981) provides a comprehensive annotated bibliography of works on all types of metre and verse form.

METAPHOR

Metaphor is derived from the Greek verb that means 'to carry over'. When words are used metaphorically, one field of reference is carried over or transferred into another. Wordsworth (in 'Resolution and Independence') states that 'The sky rejoices in the morning's birth.' He carries over two very human attributes to the non-human phenomena of the sky and the morning: the ability to rejoice and to give birth. I. A. Richards (1936) devised a formula that enables us to specify the process of carrying over. The 'tenor' of the metaphor is its principal subject, the topic addressed: in Wordsworth's line the tenor is the speaker's perception of the sky and the morning. The 'vehicle' is the analogue or the subject carried over from another field of reference to that of the subject: in Wordsworth's line the activities of rejoicing and giving birth.

Metaphor is often referred to as a poetic device but it is not exclusive to poetry. Metaphors will be found in newspaper articles on economics: 'The war [vehicle] against inflation [tenor]'; in ordinary conversation: 'At yesterday's meeting [tenor] I broke the ice [vehicle]'; in novels: 'He cowered in the shadow [vehicle] of the thought [tenor]' (James Joyce's *A Portrait of the Artist as a Young Man*); and in advertisements: 'This car is as good on paper [vehicle] as it is on the road [tenor]'.

The principal difference between Wordsworth's metaphor and its non-poetic counterparts is its integration with the iambic pentameter.

The sky | rējoíc | ēs iń | thē mórn | iñg's bírth.

We could retain the metaphor and lose the metre; turn it into the kind of unmetrical sentence that might open a short story or a novel: 'I watched the sky rejoice in the birth of the morning.' One thing lost is the way in which the pentameter organizes and emphasizes the tenor and vehicle of the metaphor – sky rējóicēs and mórniñg's bírth. In order to properly consider differences between poetic and non-poetic uses of metaphor we should add a third element to tenor and vehicle: the ground of the metaphor (see Leech, 1969: 151). The ground is essentially the context and motivation of the metaphor. For the journalist the ground of the metaphor is the general topic of economics and inflation and the particular point that he/she is attempting to make about these issues. For the conversationalist the ground is the awareness, shared with the addressee, of yesterday's meeting and his/her role in it. For the advertiser the ground involves the rest of the advertisement, giving details of the make, price and performance of the car, and the general context in which cars are discussed and sold. In non-poetic uses of metaphor the ground or context stabilizes the relation between tenor and vehicle. The metaphor will involve a self-conscious departure from the routine and familiar relationship between language and reality. It would be regarded as bizarre and mildly disturbing if the conversationalist were to allow the original metaphor to dominate the rest of his/her discourse: 'I sank through the broken ice into the cold water of the boardroom. There we all were: fishes swimming through a dark hostile world . . .'.

In poems, however, this relation between ground, tenor and vehicle is often reversed. It is the language of the poem, as much as the reader's *a priori* knowledge, which creates its perceived situation and context. It constructs its own ground, and metaphor becomes less a departure from contextual terms and conditions and more a device which appropriates and even establishes them. In John Donne's 'The Flea' the tenor is the insect itself and the bite it has inflicted on the male speaker and the female listener. The speaker carries over this tenor into such an enormous diversity of vehicles that it becomes difficult to distinguish between the ground outside the words of the text and the ground which the text appropriates and continually transforms.

> This flea is you and I, and this
> Our marriage bed and marriage temple is.

We know that 'this flea' is the tenor, but the relation between tenor and ground becomes less certain with 'is you and I'. On the one hand it is literally part of them since it has sucked and mixed their blood. On the other the speaker has already incorporated this image of physical unity into a vehicle involving their emotional and sexual lives. He builds on this with the vehicle of the 'marriage bed' and extends it into an image of spiritual, external unity in the 'marriage temple'. Throughout the poem the flea and the bite become gradually detached from their actual context and threaded into a chain of speculative and fantastic associations.

In ordinary language metaphor usually stands out from the rest of the discursive or factual nature of the statement. In poetry a particular use of metaphor will often underpin and influence the major themes of the entire text. Donne's 'The Ecstasy' opens with a simile (the bank 'is like' a pillow, rather than 'is' a pillow) but thereafter maintains a close, metaphoric, relation between tenor and vehicle,

> Where, like a pillow on a bed,
>   A pregnant bank swelled up to rest
> The violet's reclining head
>   Sat we two, one another's best;

The tenor is the garden in which 'we two' are situated; the vehicle is a combination of images denoting intimacy and sexuality: pillow, bed, pregnant, swelled up, the violets (flower, denoting female) reclining head. This opening instance of the carrying over of rural horticultural images into the sphere of human sexuality becomes the predominant theme of the entire poem, underpinning more adventurous speculations on the nature of the soul. Again the dynamics of contrasting and associating verbal images has unsettled the stabilizing function of ground or context.

Donne is one of the so-called metaphysical school of poetic writers whose taste for extended metaphor is a principal characteristic of their verse, but the practice of creating tensions and associations between the words and images of the poem at the expense of an external context transcends schools, fashions and historical groupings.

In Keats's 'Ode to a Nightingale' the image of the real bird becomes a springboard for a complex sequence of associations and resonances: song, poetry, immortality, age, youth, death. The sense of there being a specific place and time in which Keats saw the bird and heard its song is gradually replaced by the dynamics of Keats's associative faculties: the relation between the vehicles unsettles the relation between vehicle and tenor. The following is from the beginning of stanza 3:

> Fade far away, dissolve, and quite forget
>> What thou among the leaves hast never known,
> The weariness, the fever, and the fret
>> Here, where men sit and hear each other groan;

The principal vehicle is Keats's transformation of the bird into an apparently ratiocinative, cognitive addressee, who understands his words. This at the same time is unsettled by his constant return to the commonsense tenor of a bird without human faculties. The dynamic tension here becomes evident in Keats's contradictory request that the nightingale should 'forget' those human qualities or frailties which, as he concedes in the next line, it had never and could never have known.

A classic case of vehicle undermining tenor occurs in T. S. Eliot's 'The Love Song of J. Alfred Prufrock' (lines 15–22). This begins with the tenor (the city fog) being carried over into the vehicle of an unspecified animal which 'rubs its back upon the window-panes', 'rubs its muzzle on the window-panes', 'Licked its tongue into the corners of the evening'. By the end of the passage the actual vision of city streets which inspired the comparison has been overtaken by the physical presence of this strange beast, which 'seeing that it was a soft October night, / Curled once about the house, and fell asleep'.

Metaphor is the most economical, adventurous and concentrated example of the general principle of 'carrying over'. Samuel Johnson defined metaphor in his *Dictionary* (1755) as 'a simile compressed in a word'. Donne's metaphor (from 'The Relic'), 'a bracelet of bright hair about the bone', would, as a simile, be something like: 'the brightness of the hair about the bone reminds me of the difference between life and death'. Simile postulates the comparison: X is like Y. Metaphor synthesizes the comparison: X *is* Y. Metonymy is logical metaphor, in which the comparison is founded upon an actual, verifiable relation between objects or impressions: 'crown' is used instead of 'king', 'queen' or 'royalty'. Allegory involves an extended parallel between a narrative and a subtext which mirrors the relation between the text and reality. Spenser's *The Faerie Queen* (1590–6) is a medieval fantasy with allegorical parallels in the real world of the Elizabethan court.

Simile, metonymy and allegory establish a balanced relationship between the use of language and conventional perceptions of reality, and occur as frequently in non-poetic discourse as in poetry. Metaphor involves language in an unbalancing of perceptions of reality and is more closely allied to the experimental character of poetry.

SYNTAX, DICTION AND VOCABULARY

The terms 'poetic diction' and 'poetic syntax' should be treated with caution. Any word, clause, phrase, grammatical habit or locution used in non-poetic language can be used in poetry. But their presence within the poem will subtly alter their familiar non-poetic function. For example, in Donne's 'The Flea' the speaker reflects upon the likely objections to his proposal to the woman:

> Though parents grudge, and you, we are met
> And cloistered in these living walls of jet.

We might explain the use of the phrase 'and you' as a result of hurried and improvised speech. ('Though you and your parents grudge' would be a more correct form.) But the fact that the placing of the phrase maintains the movement of the iambic metre and the symmetry of the two lines of the couplet shows us that the speech is anything but improvised.

The metrical structure of a poem can accommodate the

apparent hesitations and spontaneities of ordinary speech, but at the same time fix them as parts of a carefully structured artefact. Consider what happens when syntax crosses the space between two poetic lines, an effect known as enjambment. A classic example of this occurs in the opening lines of Milton's *Paradise Lost*:

> Of Man's first disobedience, and the fruit
> Of that forbidden tree, whose mortal taste

The implied pause at the line ending might suggest, on Milton's part, a slight moment of indecision: is he thinking of the figurative 'fruit' (that is, the result and consequences) of man's disobedience, or the literal fruit of the act of disobedience? He chooses the latter. The placing of the word might also be interpreted as the complete opposite of fleeting indecision. The tension between the actuality of the fruit and the uncertain consequences of eating it is a fundamental theme of the poem, and Milton encodes this tension within the form of the poem even before its narrative begins.

In non-poetic language the progress of syntax can be influenced by a number of external factors: an act or verbal interruption by someone else, the uncertainty of the speaker or the fraught circumstances of the speech act: known in stylistics as the pragmatic or functional registers of language. For example, conversations often consist of broken, incomplete syntactic units because both speakers are contributing to the same discourse, which will also involve a shared non-verbal frame of reference:

> 'Look at this, its' . . . '
> 'Well, it's big enough',
> 'Whoa, sorry.'
> 'It's OK, it'll clean up.'

In poetry apparent hesitations or disturbances of syntax are a function of the carefully planned, integrated structure of the text.

The ability of poetry to absorb and recontextualize the devices and registers of non-poetic language is evident also in its use of diction, vocabulary, and phrasing. The social or local associations of particular words or locutionary habits can be carried into a poem but their familiar context will be transformed by their new structural framework. In Tony Harrison's *V* (1985) the poet converses in a Leeds cemetery with an imagined skinhead whose hobbies include the spraying of graffiti on to gravestones:

> 'Listen cunt!' I said, 'Before you start your jeering
> The reason why I want this in a book
> 's to give ungrateful cunts like you a hearing!'
> *A book, yer stupid cunts not worth a fuck.*

The diction and idiom of both speakers is working class and Northern, but this specific, locative resonance is itself contained within a separate language, with its own conventions: each regional idiomatic flourish is confidently, almost elegantly, reconciled to the demands of the iambic pentameter and the quatrain. The realistic crudity of the language is juxtaposed with the controlled irony of Harrison's formal design: the skinhead's real presence is appropriated to the unreal structure of the poem, involving the internal and external rhymes, 'book' and 'fuck'. In a broader context, the language of working-class Leeds is integrated with the same stanzaic structure used by Gray in his 'Elegy Written in a Country Churchyard', in which the poet similarly appropriates the voice of a 'hoary-headed swain'.

> Haply some hoary-headed swain may say,
> 'Oft have we seen him at the peep of dawn
> Brushing with hasty steps the dews away
> To meet the sun upon the upland lawn.

Gray's and Harrison's language and experience are centuries and worlds apart – the diction of the hoary-headed individual is rather more delicate than that of his skinheaded counterpart – but their differences are counterpointed against their enclosure within the same ahistorical stanzaic framework.

This tendency for poetry to represent and at the same time colonize the habits of non-poetic discourse is a paradox that has taxed poets and critics – most famously in Wordsworth's Preface to *Lyrical Ballads* (1798). Wordsworth rails against the stultifying poeticization of ordinary language, of how the conventions and style of eighteenth-century verse had dispossessed poetry of the 'real language of men'. But while he advocates a new kind of poetic writing he concedes that poetry must announce its difference in a way that will 'entirely separate the composition from the vulgarity and meanness of ordinary life'. In short, although poetry should be about 'ordinary life' it must by its very nature be separate from it. D. H. Lawrence's poems in the Nottinghamshire dialect, Robert Burns's and Hugh MacDiarmid's use of Scots idiom, grammar and diction emphasize region and very often class, but no matter where the words come from or what social or political affiliations they carry, they are always appropriated and acted upon by the internal structures of poetry.

Wordsworth's desire to separate poetry from the 'vulgarity and meanness of ordinary life' sounds suspiciously elitist and exclusive, and there is evidence of this in the work of a number of our most celebrated poets. In Part II of *The Waste Land* (1922) Eliot represents the speech patterns and, so he assumes, the concerns of working-class women:

> Now Albert's coming back, make yourself a bit smart.
> He'll want to know what you done with that money he gave you
> To get yourself some teeth.

We will be expected to note the difference between this passage and the sophisticated command of metre and multicultural references of the poem's principal male voice, Tiresias. With whom would we associate T. S. Eliot? Tiresias or the women?

The sense of poetry as carrying social and political allegiances (principally male, white, English, middle class, educated) has prompted acts of stylistic revolution. William Carlos Williams in the free verse of *Spring and All* and *Paterson* (1946–58) effectively discards those conventions of rhyme and metre that restrict his use of ordinary American phrasing and vocabulary (see pp. 154–7 for examples). Linton Kwesi Johnson makes the structure of his poems respond to the character of his language.

> But love is
> just a word;
> give it MEANIN
> thru HACKSHAN.

'MEANIN' and 'HACKSHAN' are words appropriated from 'standard' English by West Indians, and the fact that Johnson has used poetry to emphasize their ownership is significant. The unusual concentrations and foregroundings of poetry can unsettle just as much as they can underpin the allegiances and ideologies of diction and vocabulary.

CRITICAL METHODS

So far I have considered three principal characteristics of poetry and the extent to which they contribute to stylistics: metre and prosody; metaphor; diction and vocabulary. In doing so I have maintained a degree of continuity with rhetoric: I have listed, documented, defined and specified. One of the main differences between the stylistics of modern criticism and rhetoric is that modern critics have been especially interested in showing how these different elements combine to produce effects that are unique to poems. In what follows I shall consider examples of how textualist critics have attempted to cross the divide between the documentation of style and the description of uniquely poetic effects.

In the first chapter of *Seven Types of Ambiguity* (1930) William Empson discusses the ways in which the sound patterns of poetry create a fabric of meaning which can both supplement and deviate from the conventional structures of grammar, syntax and semantics. At one point he considers an extract from Browning.

> I want to know a butcher paints,
> A baker rhymes for his pursuit,
> Candlestick-maker much acquaints
> His soul with song, or, haply mute,
> Blows out his brains upon the flute.

Empson observes that the stanza is ambiguous in that it connotes at least three levels of meaning. He notes their operations in the first line.

> I want to know what the whole class of butchers paints,
>
> I want to know what some one butcher paints,
>
> I want to know personally a butcher who paints.

Empson comments: 'The demands of metre allow the poet to say something which is not normal colloquial English, so that the reader thinks of the colloquial forms which are near to it, and puts them together; weighing their probabilities in proportion to their nearness. It is for such reasons as this that poetry can be more compact, while seeming to be less precise, than prose' (from reprint in Lodge, 1972: 56).

His argument is founded upon two principles: (1) Metre and rhyme provide a system of organization which centralizes what, in prose, would be unfocused; (2) Unlike in prose, where we attempt to resolve the ambiguity into a specific referential meaning, we should regard poetic ambiguity as an element of dynamic meaning.

Cleanth Brooks, in another classic of textualist stylistics, *The Well Wrought Urn* (1947), employs a similar method in relation to poetic paradox. The following is his discussion of the closing two lines of Wordsworth's sonnet 'Composed Upon Westminster Bridge':

> Dear God! the very houses seem asleep;
> And all that mighty heart is lying still!
>
> To say they are 'asleep' is to say they are alive, that they participate in the life of nature . . . . It is only when the poet sees the city under the semblance of death [heart is lying still] that he can see it as actually alive.

> (Lodge, 1972: 294)

Brooks regards the entire poem as underpinned by a fundamental set of paradoxes (principally, awake/asleep, life/death). In ordinary language we attempt to distinguish between them; in poetry they are stylistically telescoped into delicate nuances of contrast and combination.

Empson's and Brooks's practice is a mode of stylistic criticism that is summed up in the following way in a book by Brooks and Robert Penn Warren, called *Understanding Poetry* (1938: 26–7):

> [the poet] cannot assemble them [an episode, a metaphor, a phrase, a metrical device] in a merely arbitrary fashion; they must bear some relation to each other. So he develops his sense of the whole . . . it modifies the process by which the poet selects and relates the parts, the words, images, rhythms, local ideas, events etc. . . . It is an infinitely complicated process of establishing interrelations.

This model of poetic structure positions the poet as the pivot between the stylistic features that define poetry and the broader network of relations between language and meaning. The poet will both dispose language in order to construct a formal unity within the text, and establish 'interrelations' between this structural entity and the real world. The theoretical underpinnings of this thesis are explored in two seminal New Critical essays, John Crowe Ransom's 'Criticism Inc.' (1937) and W. K. Wimsatt and

M. Beardsley's 'The Intentional Fallacy' (in Wimsatt, 1954). Ransom accepts that the topics and issues found in literary texts, such as sex, God, politics and social mores, are the subjects of academic disciplines such as history, sociology and philosophy. He argues that literary criticism is different from these because it is as much concerned with the processes of stylistic refraction as it is with the topics and ideas mediated by the literary text. Wimsatt and Beardsley promote the same premise in their examination of the linguistic and situational elements of intention. They assert that the non-literary concept of intention, in which the linguistic declaration is rooted in verifiable conditions and circumstances, is invalid and fallacious in literary criticism. The speaker of the poem is not the channel for an intended message; rather, speaker, circumstances, conditions and message are variously constructed and distorted by the stylistic fabric of the poem. Keats's 'Ode to a Nightingale' involves a speaker and a speech act. A non-poetic speech act might involve similar uncertainties, contradictions and irregularities, and we would attempt to resolve these by predicating them upon an assumed intention on the part of the speaker to deliver a particular message for a particular reason. Wimsatt and Beardsley, and Ransom, would argue that the uncertainties and ambiguities of Keats's speech act should not be resolved or paraphrased in terms of the actual intention or set of circumstances that might have precipitated them. On the contrary, these uncertainties should be seen as a continuous, unresolvable interplay of potential intentions and meanings, detached from the causal relation between thought and expression in non-poetic language.

New Critical stylistics is concerned not only with the identification of linguistic features that make poetry different from other discourses, but with poetry as a form of signification which mysteriously transforms the familiar relationship between language and meaning. I. A. Richards, whose definition of metaphor we have already considered, insists that although his terminology and frame of reference are founded upon non-literary linguistics, the effects produced by poetry are not easily reducible to predictable, scientific models of language. He qualifies his distinction between vehicle (device) and tenor (meaning): 'the vehicle is not normally a mere embellishment of a tenor which is otherwise unchanged by it but . . . vehicle and tenor in cooperaton give a meaning of more varied powers than can be ascribed to either' (1936: 100). In short when vehicle and tenor are combined the relation between the meanings of the words used becomes more significant than the relation between each word and its specific meaning.

Roman Jakobson is a critic who has combined the New Critics' respect for the refractory mysteries of poetic language with a far more rigorous programme of linguistic analysis. Jakobson began his work on linguistics and poetry during the Formalist heyday between 1900 and the 1920s, but the Anglo-American branch of literary studies only became fully aware of his ideas on the publication of his 1960 paper, 'Closing Statement: Linguistics and Poetics', which incorporates the most significant elements of fifty years' work on both topics.

Jakobson's model of language is founded upon Saussure's thesis that there are three levels of interaction between language and meaning: signifier (the visual or phonemic substance of the word); signified (the concept or image represented by the word); referent (the pre-linguistic object or condition).

Jakobson, again drawing upon Saussure, developed a systematic framework for the analysis of the signifier–signified relationship within the broader structures of language. This involves a continuous tension between what he calls the combinative and the selective axes of language and provides the basis for his most quoted and widely debated definition of poetry, the projection principle: 'The poetic function projects the principle of equivalence from the axis of selection into the axis of combination' (1988: 39; first pub. 1960). These two axes can be represented as follows:

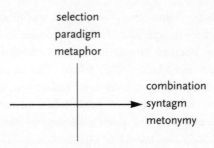

selection
paradigm
metaphor

combination
syntagm
metonymy

The axis of combination involves the system of rules and conventions (grammar and syntax) through which individual words are combined into larger units of meaning – the dominant, all-purpose unit of combination being the sentence, or in Jakobson's terms the syntagmatic chain. The axis of selection involves the choices made at each stage in the syntagm from the different words available for each grammatical class or type – in Jakobson's terms paradigmatic selection. For example, in order to describe the progress of a person along the street we might use different verbs to describe the same activity: the person walks; strolls; moves; strides – we can choose different verbs from the selective axis while maintaining the same syntagmatic-combinative formula (article–noun–verb).

The principle of equivalence involves the matching of the two axes; first in terms of the rules of the syntagmatic chain ('Its person is walk' is grammatically incorrect), and secondly in terms of the agreed or 'equivalent' relation between the rules of the syntagm and the perceived relation between language (signifier and signified) and the pre-linguistic world (the referent). If I stated that 'A tree walks' I would have satisfied the rules of the syntagm ('walks', like 'grows' or 'lives' is a verb used in its correct grammatical position), but I would have disrupted the perceived or equivalent relation between language and the pre-linguistic world: trees as far as we know cannot and do not walk. This unusual and unexpected use of the selective axis is the basic principle of metaphor.

Jakobson claims that 'for poetry, metaphor – and for prose metonymy – is the line of least resistance and consequently the study of poetical tropes is directed chiefly toward metaphor' (Jakobson and Halle, 1956: 95–6). This does not mean that all prosaic language is metonymic; rather that metonymy is more indicative of the logic of prose while metaphor embodies the fundamental illogic of poetry. Metonymy involves a comparison between two conditions or elements that have a pre-established connection in the empirical world. We frequently refer to elements of monarchial government in terms of 'the crown' (crown forces, crown lands, etc.); and we might refer to a person's car as 'her wheels'. Metonymy involves the substitution of one element of an object or condition for its entirety; and, as Jakobson argues, it embodies the governing principle of prosaic, non-poetic language: that language should reflect and articulate the perceived condition of the external world. Metaphor, conversely, uses the selective axis to variously disrupt and refocus the perceived relation between language and reality. In Donne's 'The Flea', the speaker effects a number of radical shifts from the logic of metonymy to the more adventurous illogic of metaphor.

THE FLEA

Mark but this flea, and mark in this,
How little that which thou deny'st me is;
Me it sucked first, and now sucks thee,
And in this flea, our two bloods mingled be;
Confess it, this cannot be said
A sin, or shame, or loss of maidenhead,
    Yet this enjoys before it woo,
    And pampered swells with one blood made of two,
    And this, alas, is more than we would do.

Oh stay, three lives in one flea spare,
Where we almost, nay more than married are:

This flea is you and I, and this
Our marriage bed, and marriage temple is;
Though parents grudge, and you, we are met,
And cloistered in these living walls of jet.
 Though use make thee apt to kill me,
 Let not to this, self murder added be,
 And sacrilege, three sins in killing three.

Cruel and sudden, hast thou since
Purpled thy nail, in blood of innocence?
In what could this flea guilty be,
Except in that drop which it sucked from thee?
Yet thou triumph'st and say'st that thou
Find'st not thyself, nor me the weaker now;
 'Tis true, then learn how false, fears be;
 Just so much honour, when thou yield'st to me,
 Will waste, as this flea's death took life from thee.

In the first stanza the speaker combines verifiable fact (the flea has bitten both of them) with broader issues of sexual morality (a sin, or shame, or loss of maidenhead); and in the second stanza the logic of metonymy is transformed into the persuasive anti-logic of metaphor. The literal combining of blood becomes the figurative, metaphoric image of 'three lives' and 'more than married'; the actual mixing of their physical presences (this flea is you and I) is transmuted into a compound metaphor involving their 'marriage' bed and temple, religious symbolism ('*cloistered* in these living walls of jet'), and the literal and figurative 'murder' of their relationship. This procedure involves a gradual shift from the axis of combination, in which words are combined according to the logical, functional meaning (the flea bite and the literal mixing of their blood) towards an extended metaphor in which the discourse is dominated by the selection of words which create new and unexpected levels of meaning.

The continuous and persistent use of metaphor in a text does not automatically define it as a poem. As Jakobson argues, 'The principle of similarity underlies poetry; the metrical parallelism of lines or the phonic equivalence of rhyming words prompts the question of semantic similarity or contrast; there exist, for instance, grammatical and antigrammatical but never agrammatical rhymes' (1987:114). Along with their projection of the axis of selection into the axis of combination (metaphor), poems also create a continuous level of interference between poetic form (metre, rhyme, assonance and alliteration) and the practical, non-poetic registers of syntax and semantics. Consider the way in which the internal and external rhymes of 'The Flea' tend to fix our attention on the tenor (the flea and flea bite) of the metaphor: 'this flea', 'in this' 'me is', 'Me', 'thee', 'be', 'This flea', 'and this', 'temple is', 'kill me', 'added be', 'killing three', 'guilty be', 'from thee', 'fears be', 'to me', 'from thee'. The principal themes of the speaker's argument are drawn into a network of semantic and phonetic associations – mainly 'this flea' 'is' 'thee' 'be' 'me' – that creates an almost subliminal counterpart to the metaphor. As Jakobson states, the logical meaning of the words of a poem is tied into a system of phonemic and rhythmic similarities and parallels: in this case the persuasive echoes of the rhyme scheme insinuate themselves into the rhetoric of the extended metaphor.

Jakobson's discussions of how poetry combines rhetorical devices such as metaphor with sound patterns are far more methodical, more grounded in the techniques of linguistics, than those of his New Critical counterparts. His most significant contribution to the stylistics of poetry is the application of this disciplinary rigour to the rather vague New Critical model of the relation between the poem and the non-poetic world of language and events. He writes:

> Not only the message [of poetry] but also its addresser and addressee
> become ambiguous . . . the supremacy of the poetic function over

the referential function does not obliterate the message but makes it ambiguous. The double sensed message finds correspondence in a split addresser, in a split addressee as well as in a split reference.

(1988: 50; first pub. 1960)

This sense of a split frame of reference seems to correspond with Empson's and Brooks's notions of ambiguity and paradox, but Jakobson's model is far more comprehensive, in that it is founded upon a model of linguistic interaction which, he claims, underpins all speech acts. He represents this in a diagram.

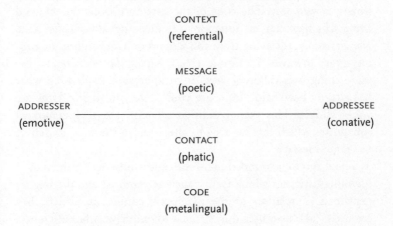

CONTEXT
(referential)

MESSAGE
(poetic)

ADDRESSER   ADDRESSEE

(emotive)   (conative)

CONTACT
(phatic)

CODE
(metalingual)

The parts of the diagram in upper-case letters refer mainly to the physical and contextual elements of any act of verbal communication. The CONTEXT in which the act takes place will influence the degree of CONTACT between ADDRESSER and ADDRESSEE. All of these will affect the nature of the MESSAGE and the form or style in which the message is delivered, its CODE. In turn, these physical and contextual factors will influence the parts of the diagram in brackets, which refer mainly to the actual structure and meaning of the language in a particular act of communication.

If we speak on the telephone we generally need to establish that the addresser is who we expect him/her to be. Consequently this establishment of a contact function will cause us to use phatic utterances (i.e. not specifically related to the meaning or intention of the message) that would be unnecessary in face-to-face exchanges ('Hello! Is that you?'). The context of the speech act can alter its code. If at a dinner table we ask our new boss whether he/she is enjoying the meal we are unlikely to use the same code as the one employed to deliver the same enquiry over the breakfast table to our partner of twenty years, or our grouchy three-year-old son. The code of the utterance is changeable and these changes are a function of metalingual transferences. Metalanguage (deriving from the same root as metaphor – carrying over) involves, in simple terms, saying or referring to the same thing in a different way, or paraphrasing, explaining what has already been said. 'How are you?', 'Are you well?', 'How are you feeling?', 'Has your condition altered?' are all metalingual substitutes which involve a slight alteration in the code to deliver the same message.

The diagram is founded upon the cause-and-effect principles of sociolinguistics, in which factors such as grammar and diction are explained in relation to the pragmatic context in which they are used. Jakobson uses this formula to emphasize the difference, the split, between poetic and non-poetic language, and crucial to this is his pairing of message with poetic.

In 'The Flea' there are linguistic elements that relate to all of the contextual influences of ordinary language. At the beginning of stanza 2 the phrase 'Oh stay' depends for its meaning upon a general awareness of its context. This phrase is prompted as much by the unpredictable immediacy of the speech act (the addresser in stanza 1 cannot predict that the addressee will attempt to squash the flea) as it is by any prepared code for the delivery of the intended message (his request for sex). At the same time, however, the actuality of the situation in which the words are used, what we call the 'ground', is disrupted by the fact that while it is possible to recreate the context of the utterance from the words it is impossible to imagine that any addresser in any real situation would have any reason, let alone the time and ability, to incorporate 'Oh stay' as the opening iamb in an octosyllabic line, which in turn is locked into a complex, thrice-repeated stanzaic pattern.

Jakobson uses linguistics to validate the general thesis that poetry is different from ordinary language, not simply in its stylistic devices but in the way that these devices create patterns within a text which isolate that text from the normal cause-and-effect relationship between language and its context – the 'split'. Empson, in his attempt to contextualize Browning's poem on the butcher, reduces the lines to three potential metalinguistic substitutes. He treats them as we would an uncertain or ambiguous message delivered by a real addresser, and concludes, rather obliquely, 'that poetry can be more compact, while seeming to be less precise, than prose'. Empson and Brooks approach the poetic text in terms of the normal, contextual conditions of non-poetic language, in the sense that they occupy the position of the addressee and attempt to make sense of the stylistic excesses of the addresser (poet and poetic persona). Jakobson alters this formula and argues that whenever the poetic function is combined with the message an ambiguity or split permeates not only the style of the text, but also the phenomenological status of its context, its speaker (addresser) and its hearer or reader (addressee). In order to understand 'The Flea' in basic terms, we as readers need to imagine the situation created by the words, but we also become aware that this situation and its participants are patently unreal, that the poetic function (the projection principle, metre, rhyme) permeates both the words of the text and the situational context which prompts and permits a proper understanding of these words.

Jakobson's concept of the split specifies, but does not resolve, a problem that is central to the stylistics of poetry. Criticizing poetry, either in an essay or in conversation, involves a form of translation. We discuss poems in the way that we discuss politics or gardening. Our language is prosaic: we refer methodically to items, facts, devices, effects, apparent meanings. Criticism is normative; it reduces the oddities of poetic structure to the pragmatics of ordinary discourse. In Jakobson's terms we replace the unique, all-inclusive code of the poetic function with the meta-linguistic substitute of prose, explication, paraphrase. A number of modern critics use the term 'naturalization' to describe this process, and I will consider this usage in more detail in Chapter 11, on Modernism.

The problem of how to bridge this divide between what poetry is and how we discuss it has itself divided the study of poetic style. A number of critics have extended and further investigated the work of Jakobson and the New Critics. Samuel Levin (1962, 1971) set about naming and documenting those elements of poetry which exist on either side of Jakobson's 'split'. The 'cognitive' features of any text or speech act – in short the meaning-generating elements such as syntax, lexis, semantics, phonemics, shared by all linguistics discourses – are the salient structures which enable us to attain a basic level of understanding. The 'conventional' features are those that poetry does not share with other discourses, especially its division into lines, with sub-divisions consisting of metrical pattern, rhyme scheme and sound pattern. Levin coins the term 'coupling' to describe instances in which these two dimensions interact. The couplings of the cognitive and conventional features of 'The Flea' are complex and continuous.

Levin's formula provides a useful means of documenting the active constituents of poetic style, but it begs the question of how exactly the meanings created by coupling are different from stylistic cruces and paraphrasable meanings of ordinary language. For example Pope begins his 'Epistle to Dr Arbuthnot' (1735) with the couplet:

Shut, shut the door good John! fatigu'd I said,
Tye up the knocker, say I'm sick, I'm dead.

In Levin's terms the conventional element of this couplet is the semantic contrast between the rhyme words 'said' (living speech) and 'dead' (terminal silence) and is itself underpinned by the metrical symmetry of the two lines. The operation of the conventional features injects a supplementary level of sardonic wit into a cognitive message that could be paraphrased as weary hyperbole.

The problem with Levin's concept of coupling is that it will always occur in every couplet of Pope's poem. Each pair of rhyme words will create a semantic contrast that will not occur in unrhymed language, but not all of the couplets will produce the same level of conventional–cognitive interaction as the first. We can draw up an abstract model of cognitive features (how the semantic properties of words relate to their grammatical class and how the rules of syntax organize these classes) and their conventional counterparts (the metrical pattern of the iambic pentameter and the a a b b rhyme scheme of the couplet), but it would require a computer, rather than a human reader, to note, register and absorb every point of interaction of these two elements.

Michael Riffaterre (1966) was the first critic to draw attention to the potential discrepancy between our ability to document the minutiae of stylistic interaction and the ability of the average reader to appreciate that all of these things are happening at the same time. Riffaterre coined the term 'Superpoem' to account for the immensely complex phenomena disclosed by the work of Jakobson, Levin and other linguist-critics, and he invented the notion of a 'Superreader' to account for a putative and very unreal presence who is capable of accommodating these effects simultaneously, along with an *ex cathedra* knowledge of who the poet is, and how this particular poem relates to work by the same poet and by other writers.

The question of how the reader responds to, perhaps even influences, perceptions of style and effect will be dealt with in the section on contextualism (Chapter 5).

I will close this chapter by introducing a formula which helps us to more clearly define the stylistic devices and interpretive problems discussed so far: the double pattern. In simple terms the double pattern concerns the relationship between those features of the poem which are exclusive to poetic writing and those which the poem shares with other linguistic discourses. With regard to Jakobson's diagram, half of the double pattern consists of the six linguistic and situational elements of any statement (addresser, addressee, context, message, contact, code). The other half is the effect upon these when each is informed by the consistent use of a poetic device. On the one hand the diction and phrasing of Donne's 'The Flea' preserve all of the characteristics of an improvised statement delivered by a male addresser around the beginning of the seventeenth century. On the other the imagined situation of a man addressing a woman in a real situation involving the contingent elements of context, contact and code is made unreal by the unimprovised metrical and rhyming symmetries of the text. Levin's distinction between the cognitive (non-poetic) and conventional (poetic) features of the text enables us to specify the linguistic causes of the double pattern, but of more significance is its effect upon our ability to reconcile the stylistic character of the poem with a perceived intention or context.

Let us compare the following two extracts. The first is the opening stanza of Dylan Thomas's 'When, Like a Running Grave' and the second is the first four lines of John Gould Fletcher's 'Irradiations'.

When, like a running grave, time tracks you down,
Your calm and cuddled is a scythe of hairs,
Love in her gear is slowly through the house,
Up naked stairs, a turtle in a hearse,
Hauled to the dome,

> Flickering of incessant rain
> On flashing pavements:
> Sudden scurry of umbrellas:
> Bending, recurved blossoms of the storm.

Thomas's stanza consists of four slightly irregular iambic pentameters followed by a four-syllable line, and has an a b b b a pattern of off-rhymes. A sequence of assonantal and alliterative patterns stands in oblique relation to the metre and the rhyme scheme. The format is repeated in each of the poem's ten stanzas.

This dense and intrinsic network of stress and sound creates a pattern of echoes and parallels along the syntagmatic chain and deflects our attempts to go through the surface structure to paraphrase its meaning. These difficulties are increased by the multilayering of figures and tropes. The ground, the referential anchor for Thomas's figures, is constantly unsettled by the complexity of the figures themselves. The 'you' of the first line is not identified either as a particular person or as a metonymic substitute for the universal condition of humanity. This presence is pursued, and caught, by time, while at the same time some type of activity, also involving the 'you', and a personified condition of 'Love' takes place in a 'house'. So far we have three personae: the you and the binary personifications of love and time. The presence of the latter pair is strengthened by a pattern of images connoting respectively life/sexuality and death/termination: 'calm and cuddled', 'scythe of hairs', 'turtle' (a traditional emblem of love); 'running grave', 'hearse/Hauled to the dome'. Apart from the tripartite relation between humanity, life and death there is no concrete or secure ground for the tenor–vehicle dynamics of Thomas's metaphors: the images are thematically related to each other but they are not carried over from an identifiable context.

Unlike in Donne's 'The Flea' (see above pp. 38–9) where there is a constant distinction between the metrical pattern, the speaker's ingenious use of metaphor and imagery (in Levin's terms the conventional level) and the actuality of the situation and the personae of the text (the cognitive level), in Thomas's poem any clear perception of the latter is continuously absorbed and dissipated by the complexities of the former.

One could argue that the poetic, conventional element of the double pattern has effectively replaced the cognitive function of syntax. The relative adverb 'When' which begins the stanza has no particular subject; rather the rest of the syntagm switches from the conditional future to the closely observed present ('*is* a scythe . . .', '*is* slowly' rather than 'will be' or 'will'); and this uncertain relation between temporal registers and sub- and main clauses is not resolved in subsequent stanzas. The unfixed syntax stands in contrast to the relative precision of the metrical and rhyming framework. What in prose form might read as incoherent nonsense is provided with a thread of continuity by the carefully repeated stanzaic structure.

Fletcher's lines, conversely, are stripped of practically any element of the conventional dimension that would obstruct an impression of immediacy and spontaneity. The verbs ('Flickering', 'flashing', 'scurry', 'Bending') are without pronoun and adverb supplements ('There is . . .', 'It is . . .'). The division between the lines is determined not by an arbitrary metrical or sound pattern but by the specified frame of reference of each consecutive image. While Thomas's syntax is enveloped in a recurring metrical structure, Fletcher's is determined by an apparent desire for transparency. The only figurative usage is 'blossoms', a tenor–vehicle relation (umbrellas are like blossoming flowers) firmly embedded in the ground of the discourse. Indeed the progression of concrete images – flickering rain, flashing pavements, scurry of umbrellas – seems designed to replicate its pre-linguistic counterpart, both in the sequence perceived by the addresser and in the addresser's mental and linguistic ordering of the sequence. The rain causes the opening of umbrellas and this consecutive process settles in the mind of the perceiver prior to his metaphoric act of carrying over the immediate observations into a memory of blossoming flowers.

Thomas and Fletcher press the relation between the two halves of the double pattern to opposing extremes. Thomas embeds any pragmatic, situational register in a dynamic network of stylistic devices; Fletcher obliges the formal and syntactic element of the text to conform to and reflect the external conditions that prompted it.

Thomas's text belongs to the traditional, pre-modernist technique of constantly creating a tension between the two halves of the double pattern – although in this instance tension gives way to a surrender by one half to the other. Fletcher writes as part of the modernist rebellion against the arbitrary presence of formal structure. He promotes situational context and pre-linguistic impression as the primary determinants of style, developments which will be covered in more detail in Part II. They represent extremities, and they also illustrate the interpretive benefits of the double pattern.

Poems from all stages in literary history show a dynamic interface between the two halves of the double pattern. The conventional dimension has been altered by developments in literary history – Fletcher's mode of free verse was largely unknown before 1900 – but it is also ahistorical. A gregarious stylist such as W. H. Auden can deploy metrical structures that have been used, discarded and invented in every period from the sixteenth century to the 1970s. The cognitive dimension is more firmly rooted in the habits and frames of reference of contemporary discourse. Christopher Marlowe's iambic pentameter

> How am I glutted with conceit of this
>
> > (from *Doctor Faustus*, 1604)

and Philip Larkin's

> Not quite your class, I'd say, dear, on the whole.
>
> > (from 'Lines on a Young Lady's Photograph Album', 1955)

involve usages and locutions that are self-evidently contemporary – 'conceit' is now rarely substituted for 'the idea'; and 'on the whole' would have been unknown in 1604. However three and a half centuries of locutionary change do not alter the task of both poets in adapting their language to the configurations of five iambic feet.

Every act of poetic writing is influenced by the two dimensions of the double pattern. The poet is obliged to consider the accumulated conventions of style that constitute the existing canon of poems: which metrical forms should he/she employ, adapt or discard? At the same time he/she is working with a linguistic framework informed by the locutionary habits and frames of reference of the contemporary world. We will consider these confluences in more detail in Part II, and a fuller account of the double pattern will be found in Bradford (1993, 1994).

4

TEXTUALISM II: THE NOVEL

This chapter begins with a survey of general theories of fictional narrative, starting with the European Formalists and structuralists, Viktor Shklovsky, Vladimir Propp, A. J. Greimas and Tzvetan Todorov, and moving on to the Anglo-American literary-linguists, Booth, Chatman, Leech and Short. The next section considers Genette's theory of diegesis and focalization as a focus for attempts to document the relation between the narrator and the broader fabric of the novel. The chapter concludes with a consideration of the function of speech and dialogue in the fictional text.

MODELS OF NARRATIVE

Jakobson claims that 'for poetry metaphor, and for prose metonymy is the line of least resistance' (Jakobson and Halle, 1956: 96). In poetry, he argues, metaphoric language is constantly distorting and refracting familiar relations between words and things. Prose is more closely allied to metonymy, in that its linguistic selections maintain a parallel relationship between what is said or written and what is represented. Novels are made of prose. They are made of different types and classes of prose – formal description, meditative reflection, speech, dialogue, letters – but at a local level each different stylistic register is likely to have more in common with the functional, metonymic dimension of style than with the perversities of poetry. Consequently, the stylistics of prose fiction, while giving due attention to localized effects, is particularly concerned with the ways in which the different registers and forms of prose can be assembled as a single text which tells a story and which establishes a certain mode of formal coherence.

The two Formalists who have made the most significant contributions to subsequent theories of fiction and narrative are Viktor Shklovsky and Vladimir Propp.

Shklovsky (1917) reduced fictional structures to two opposing and interactive dimensions: *sjuzet* and *fabula*. *Fabula* refers to the actuality and the chronological sequence of the events that make up the narrative; and *sjuzet* to the order, manner and style in which they are presented in the novel in question. The *fabula* of Dickens's *Great Expectations* (1861) concerns the experiences, in and around London, from the early childhood to the adulthood of Pip. Its *sjuzet* involves the presentation of these events in Pip's first-person account of their temporal, spatial and emotional registers.

In Dickens's novel the first-person manner of the *sjuzet* has the effect of personalizing the *fabula*; Pip's description of Miss Havisham and of his relationship with Estella is necessarily influenced by factors such as his own emotional affiliations, his stylistic habits and his singular perspective on spatio-temporal sequences and conditions. If *Great Expectations* had an omniscient, third-person narrator we might learn more about the events that contributed to Miss Havisham's condition and we might be offered a more impartial multidimensional perspective on the relationship between Pip and Estella. In short, the *sjuzet* can effectively alter our perceptions of the *fabula*. Shklovsky showed a particular taste for novels which self-consciously foreground the interaction of these two elements, and his essay (1921) on Laurence Sterne's *Tristram Shandy* (1759–67) is frequently cited as an archetype of Formalist method. Throughout this novel the eponymous narrator maintains an interplay between his story (the *fabula*), and the activity and conditions of telling it (*sjuzet*). There is a close relation between Jakobson's distinction between the poetic function (the operation and effect of poetic devices) and the referential function (what the poem is about) and Shklovsky's distinction between *sjuzet* (narrative devices) and *fabula* (the story; what the novel is about).

Shklovsky and Jakobson focus on the ways in which poems and novels variously integrate and transform the non-literary registers of language and experience. Propp in *The Morphology of the Folktale* (1928) shifts our attention towards the ways in which social and behavioural structures influence and determine fictional narrative. Propp devised a grammar of the folktale based on two concepts: the roles filled by the characters (the kidnapper as villain, the princess as the kidnapped person, the king as provider, etc.) and the functions they perform in the plot. In a fairy tale several characters might be involved in a single function (the king and kidnapper might be involved in villainous activities) or one character might perform a number of functions (the king might be both hero and villain). But Propp demonstrates that there is a predictable and finite number of permutations of the role–function relation. This scheme is comparable with Jakobson's division between the syntagmatic axis of language (villain, hero, helper, etc. create narrative sequences in the same way that noun, verb and adjective create syntactic units) and its paradigmatic axis (king and hero can be substituted in certain functional roles in the same way that the verbs walk, stroll or stride are substitutable in the same place in a sentence). Both models are constrained by the agreed relation between language/narrative and perceptions of the real world. The sentence 'the tree ate its dinner and then walked home' is grammatically correct, but its paraphrasable message is implausible and absurd. Similarly a folktale in which the princess kidnaps her father, the king, in the hope of eliciting a ransom from the villain would be dismissed as absurd because its distorts the usual realm of possibilities within the social-familial network of roles and functions in the non-fictional world. Propp's model of a predictable relation between narrative structures and the social and mythological structures of the world outside the novel became the prototype for later structuralist analyses of fiction.

A. J. Greimas (1966, 1970) regards narrative patterns as involving systems of consecutive ordering very similar to the syntagm, while arguing that fictional narratives reflect the deep-rooted 'grammars' of human society: *syntagmes contractuels* – formal contracts, family bonds, close relationships, institutional ties; *syntagmes performanciels* – trials, arguments, the performance of tasks; *syntagmes disjonctionnels* – physical movements, departures, arrivals. Just as in the syntagmatic chain of a sentence each word and phrase is tied into an accumulative sequence which generates larger units of meaning, so in a novel single incidents such as marriages, commitments to specific professions and journeys are combined to produce extended narrative structures. Tzvetan Todorov in his analysis of Boccaccio's *Decameron* (1969) extends this parallel between syntax and narrative by reducing the latter to parts of speech (characters are nouns, their attributes adjectives, and their actions verbs), propositions involving one or more of the characters (A has sex with B; D divorces Y) and sequences in which a string of propositions makes up the complete narrative structure.

What is not entirely clear from the work of these Formalists and structuralists is whether they regard novels or literature in general as capable of extending and perhaps even transcending the structures of language and society, or whether the latter fully determine and dominate the former. The sense of the literary text as shifting uneasily between the localized specifics of language and the broader structures of social and personal existence poses a number of problems for stylistics. Novels, unlike poems, draw upon a variety of linguistic registers that we encounter regularly in everyday life, and they tell us stories that are often paralleled by events and narratives experienced by real people. Structuralism and linguistics have evolved a complex method-ology which enables us to deal with practically every stratum of human existence. If, like Propp, Greimas and Todorov, we attempt to adapt these overarching structures and systems to literary texts, do we demolish the long-held belief that literature is 'different' from other discourses and experiences? This prob-lematic relation between texts and contexts will be discussed in Chapter 5 on contextualism, but for the present let us return to the more practical question of whether it is possible to devise an abstract stylistic schema which can account for what happens in any given novel.

The following diagram illustrates the process of communication between the novelist and the reader. The model underpinning this was first developed by Wayne Booth (1961) and the diagram itself is taken from a book by Seymour Chatman (1978: 151).

Real	Implied				Implied	Real
→	→	(Narrator)→	(Narratee)	→	→	→
Author	Author				Reader	Reader

Real author and real reader are unproblematic: the former is the person who wrote the book and the latter is the actual reader, book in hand. The implied author and the implied reader are versions of their real counterparts. As real readers we might know all manner of things about the real biography of Dickens, but when we read his novels we begin to cross the borderline between our imagined perception of Dickens as a man and Dickens as the creator and orchestrator of fictional worlds and narratives. For example if we read a biography of Dickens and balance what we learn of his life against his presentation of lives and situations in his novels we focus on the relation between real author and implied author. However, if we focus exclusively on the particulars of one of his novels we move closer to the centre of Chatman's diagram. The narrator of Dickens's *Great Expectations* is Pip. He offers us a direct, first-person account of his life and experiences: we become his narratee. Chatman's diagram provides us with a model of the different but interrelated properties of novel reading. Compare it with the following diagram (from Leech and Short, 1981:210).

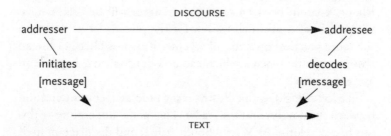

This diagram contains the principal constituents of any process of linguistic communication. DISCOURSE is linguistic communication seen as a transaction between speaker and hearer, as an interpersonal activity which is affected, sometimes determined, by its social or cultural purpose. TEXT is the unit of communication, the words transmitted from addresser to addressee. For example we can understand the text 'I need a drink' as a simple combination of pronoun, verb, indefinite article and noun, but its meaning can change radically with its context. If we know that the addresser is an alcoholic speaking to us over the phone, or someone who speaks to us from the football pitch or at the end of a marathon, the contextual circumstances will effectively determine the message of the text. Discourse is a general name for the vast network of linguistic and contextual elements that affect the 'message'.

Chatman's and Leech and Short's diagrams are founded upon a similar concept of message transference from addresser to addressee, but Chatman divides these individuals into three levels of interaction. Each of these involves a subtle shift of balance between (in Leech and Short's terms) text and discourse. The discourse between real author and real reader is affected principally by one's knowledge of the biography of the other. This can play a significant part in our perception of the style and message of the text. Emily Brontë's *Wuthering Heights* (1847), for example, was first published under the (male) pseudonym of Ellis Bell and many of its early reviewers' interpretations of the text's message were founded upon the assumption that its real author was a man (see Mary Eagleton, 1986: 71–3).

The discourse between implied author and implied reader of a particular novel will be influenced by the latter's familiarity with other novels. Chatman (1978: 148) argues that the implied author 'can *tell* us nothing . . . . It instructs us silently, through the design of the whole, with all the voices, by all the means it has chosen to let us learn.' In short, the implied author is the imagined presence which controls the style and structure of the text: the implied reader is the person who is equally conversant with this available repertoire of devices. The implied author of *Great Expectations* inhabits the space between the real author, Dickens, and the narrator, Pip. His or her field of operations includes the methods and structural devices available within the generic discourse of the novel. Dickens's implied author controls the disclosures of Pip, but the same figure might have chosen to tell the same story as a third-person narrative (Pip would be 'he' rather than 'I') or in a series of notes and letters exchanged between Pip, Miss Havisham, Estella, Magwitch and other characters who feature in the narrative.

For stylistics, the most complex and problematical relation is between narrator and narratee. There are very few novels in which the narratee is addressed directly. In *Adam Bede* (1859) George Eliot's narrator states that 'With this drop of ink at the end of my pen, I will show you [narratee] the roomy workshop of Mr. Jonathan Burge'. E. M. Forster in *Howards End* (1910: Chapter 2) has his narrator caution the narratee that 'If you think this ridiculous, remember that it is not Margaret who is telling you about it.' These are exceptions to the general convention that the narratee does not feature as an element of the text. Instead the narratee is the reader who judges the descriptions, the dialogue and reported speech of the text and its spatio-temporal structure in a way that is analogous though not identical to the way they perceive non-fictional reality. For example the narratee's encounter with the speech of a character in Chapter 6 will be affected by what he or she already knows of that character from events, descriptions and speeches earlier in the novel and by an anticipation of what the character will do later. Chatman's designation of narratee as an equal part of his six-figure diagram (p. 55) should be regarded as a concession to symmetry, since it is virtually impossible to disentangle the functions of narratee and implied reader. Both function as the recipient and decoder of the stylistic and structural patterns of the novel.

The narrator is, as we shall see, a much more complex and multifaceted individual.

GENETTE'S THEORIES OF DIEGESIS AND FOCALIZATION

Gérard Genette's *Figures III* (1972; in English *Narrative Discourse*, 1980) offers the most complete and comprehensive typology of narrators and narrative techniques, and in what follows I shall compare Genette's model with a number of other theories of fiction which variously parallel and diverge from it.

Genette classifies narrators by borrowing a term from Plato's *Republic*: diegesis. Plato distinguishes between diegesis (the story constructed by the narrator) and mimesis (speech and dialogue as a mimetic record of someone's thoughts and opinions). Genette uses diegesis as a much more comprehensive formula, which incorporates the narrator's control over the novel's characters who apparently speak or converse independently of the story. Genette's principal distinction is between what he calls the extradiegetic and the autodiegetic narrator. The extradiegetic narrator remains distant from the story, and the most obvious signal of distancing is the continuous use of the third-person account. The narrators of Henry Fielding's *Tom Jones* (1749), Honoré de Balzac's *Père Goriot* (1834) and D. H. Lawrence's *Women in Love* (1921) never refer explicitly to their own opinions or feelings or their relationship with the characters of the narrative. The third-person narrator introduces and describes characters and events (he, they, she and it, for example are third-person referring pronouns), but rarely uses the first-person 'I'. To do so would predicate involvement in the story rather than just the telling of it. The exemplary autodiegetic narrator uses the first-person pronoun and tells the story as an element of his/her own experience. Dickens's Pip and Sterne's Tristram Shandy are typically autodiegetic narrators.

Genette's main point is that although the use of stylistic signals such as first- or third-person narration can offer a superficial clue to the relation between narrator and narrative there are other more significant structural and stylistic features that can unsettle these. He argues that every kind of narrator is to some degree intradiegetic, that is to say involved in the story; the opinions, the knowledge and the style of the narrator will always have some effect upon the various elements of the narrative, no matter how much the narrator might attempt to achieve objectivity and impartiality.

D. H. Lawrence's *Women in Love* uses what on the surface is the extradiegetic form of narration. The teller seems to function only as an impersonal purveyor of the events and as a link between the spoken exchanges of the characters. But there are close stylistic resemblances between the narrator's descriptions of events and the extended spoken discourses of the main characters. This is Birkin on the personal characteristics and habits of Gudrun:

> Gudrun is rather self opinionated. She won't go cheap anywhere. Or if she does, she'll pretty soon take herself back. So whether she would condescend to do private teaching, particularly here in Beldover, I don't know. But it would be just the thing.
>
> (Chapter 16)

This is the narrator on Gudrun's circumstances and choices:

> She had a certain amount of money. She had come home partly to save, and now she had sold several pieces of work, she had been praised in various shows. She knew she could become quite the 'go' if she went to London. But she knew London, she wanted something else.
>
> (Chapter 17)

If we substitute 'Gudrun' for 'she' in the second passage and shift it from the past to the present tense it would be difficult to distinguish the stylistic characteristics of the narrator from those of his character. In both passages the pronoun/proper name operates as the tie around which a variety of referential economies and elaborations are threaded. Indeed the apparently objective narrator of the second passage and Birkin, who knows Gudrun personally, share an almost identical habit of juxtaposing facts and intrusive opinions about Gudrun's mental and emotional condition.

A close relationship between an apparently distant, extra-diegetic narrator and the condition of the novel's characters is not uncommon in third-person narratives. Jane Austen's narrator in *Northanger Abbey* (1818) describes the principal character of the novel in its opening sentences: 'No one who had ever seen Catherine Morland in her infancy, would have supposed her born to be an heroine. Her situation in life, the character of her father and mother, her own person and disposition, were all equally against her.' Throughout the novel the narrator never discloses any personal, social or familiar relation with the characters, but the first sentence is not consistent with this impression of objectivity.

The deictic features of language are those which orientate or anchor utterances in the context of space (here versus there; this versus that) or of time (now versus then), relative to the speaker's point of view. The deictics of this opening passage disclose that the narrator has detailed knowledge of Catherine's childhood, her social status, the character of her parents and of her physical and emotional condition. Indeed the first 2,000 words of the novel consist of a precise documentation of Catherine's experiences as a child, her appearance, her habits, her tastes, her talents, her relationship with her parents and her psychological make-up. Only Catherine herself or someone with whom she had had a close and candid relationship could know all of this, but Catherine is not telling her own story and if it is being told by someone who knows her so well, why does this person not feature in the narrative?

As Genette argues, and Austen demonstrates, the distinction between narrational distance and involvement is difficult to determine. Consider again Leech and Short's diagram of addresser–addressee, discourse and text (see p. 56). In most communicative instances we are able to clarify the message by making a clear distinction between the four elements, but if we regard the narrator of *Northanger Abbey* as addresser (and ourselves as addressee) they become peculiarly entangled. Throughout the novel the narrator seems to command a remarkably well-informed awareness both of what Catherine did and of what went through her mind at the time of the events described. The beginning of Chapter 9 is typical:

> The progress of Catherine's unhappiness from the events of the
> evening, was as follows. It appeared first in a general dissatisfaction

with everybody about her, while she remained in the rooms, which speedily brought on considerable weariness and a violent desire to go home. This, on arriving in Pulteney Street, took the direction of extraordinary hunger . . .

Let us try to decode this passage in terms of Leech and Short's diagram. The deictic features suggest that the narrator either accompanied Catherine from the Rooms to Pulteney Street and spoke to her about her mood or that he/she assembled this information from a number of Catherine's acquaintances. If we read on we will find that neither of these assumptions is plausible. Later in the passage the narrator tells us of how long Catherine slept and her 'first wish' on awakening. In technical terms this is a third-person narrative but at the same time his/her field of operations is that of a first-person narrator: in Genette's typology he/she is an intradiegetic narrator. On the one hand the narrator seems to be omniscient but on the other his/her range of description never moves beyond the perceptions, experiences and thoughts of Catherine.

Genette's typology of narrators is underpinned by the general principle of focalization. Focalization offers us a new perspective on the relation between the narrator and every stylistic and structural feature of the text. Focalization is the literary-critical version of the general linguistic concept of ideational meaning: the mental image generated by the words (Jakobson uses the term 'referential' to account for the same process). Open any novel at random, choose a paragraph and you, the narratee, will be engaged in focalization. Our basic linguistic competence enables us to understand what the words mean, but their grammatical, lexical and semantic functions are tied into a requirement to focalize their meaning: who is speaking? How much are we being told about the events, people or thoughts described? Is the speaker witnessing these things at the time of their occurrence? Are they a memory of past events? What is the physical location of the speaker in relation to the events described? The deictic features of language are the principal means by which statements are focalized. In the novel the status of the narrator (autodiegetic, extradiegetic, first person, third person) will often determine the manner and level of focalization, but, as we have seen from *Northanger Abbey*, there is not always a predictable and parallel relation between narrator and focalizing agent. At one level Catherine herself is the focalizer, in that the spatio-temporal dimensions of the narrative correspond with her experiences. Rimmon-Kenan (1983) refers to this as external focalizing. At another level the unidentified narrator will disclose Catherine's thoughts and feelings in a way that Catherine herself is either incapable of doing or unwilling to do in speech: "'My dear Eleanor" cried Catherine, suppressing her feelings as well as she could . . . ' (Chapter 26, Penguin edn, 1994). Rimmon-Kenan refers to this as internal focalizing, in that our attention is directed as much to the mental condition underpinning the statement as to its functional, conversational context.

At the beginning of Dickens's *Great Expectations*, the primary agent of external focalizing (the activities of Pip) is the young, inexperienced Pip, while at the same time the internal focalizing (the thoughts and feelings of Pip) of these chapters is controlled and orchestrated by the older Pip who narrates the events from a retrospective distance of about three decades. A similar but more complicated case of split focalization occurs in James Joyce's *A Portrait of the Artist as a Young Man* (1914–15), which begins as follows:

> Once upon a time and a very good time it was there was a moocow coming down along the road and this moocow that was coming down along the road met a nicens little boy named baby tuckoo . . .
>
> His father told him that story: his father looked at him through a glass: he had a hairy face.
>
> He was baby tuckoo. The moocow came down the road where Betty Byrne lived: she sold lemon platt.

The focalizing agent of this passage is the central figure of the novel, Stephen Dedalus, at this point aged about three years. The focalizer, however, is the third-person narrator, who situates these experiences in the past tense and structures them around sentence patterns. The narrator makes stylistic concessions to the disorganized mental operations of his subject (the syntactic units of the second and third paragraphs are endearingly infantile *non sequiturs*), but within 500 words the deictic features of these childhood experiences become much better orchestrated.

> The wide playgrounds were swarming with boys. All were shouting and the prefects urged them on with strong cries. The evening air was pale and chilly and after every charge and thud of the footballers the greasy leather orb flew . . .

Throughout Joyce's novel there is a constant interface between the focalizer, the narrator, and the focalizing agent, Stephen. This also happens in *Northanger Abbey* but Joyce subtly erodes the conventions that in Austen's novel maintain the distinction between the narrator and Catherine. As the narrative of *A Portrait* follows Stephen's development through sexual and emotional rites of passage and towards intellectual maturity the style of the narrator adjusts itself to the mood and aspirations of its subject. The following is from Chapter 4 in which Stephen observes a girl on a beach:

> Her slate-blue skirts were kilted boldly about her waist and dovetailed behind her. Her bosom was as a bird's, soft and slight, slight and soft as the breast of some dark-plumaged dove. But her long fair hair was girlish: and girlish, and touched with the wonder of mortal beauty, her face.

Just as the unfocused syntax of the narrator parallels the fluctuating attention span of the infant at the beginning of the novel, so this passage is consistent with the aroused sexuality and the literary ambitions of the young man. The centre of attention is the girl's clothing and body and this is stylistically 'dovetailed' into an extravagant pattern of metaphor, assonance, alliteration and parallelism that virtually satisfies Jakobson's definition of the poetic function. Unlike Catherine's narrator, who tells us what she does and then goes on to reflect upon its emotional effects, Stephen's narrator creates a stylistic representation that combines internal and external focalization. He writes in the way that, from our knowledge of Stephen, we would expect Stephen to write.

Genette's concept of focalization is important because it provides a cohesive centre for the potentially disorientating variety of stylistic techniques that have been applied in the novel. Leech and Short (1981: 70) are clear about the difficulties of arriving at a consistent and comprehensive model for the analysis of style in the novel. 'There is no complete list of the linguistic properties of a text; therefore we have to select the features to study.'

In 1977 Roger Fowler coined the term 'mind style':

> Cumulatively, consistent structural options, agreeing in cutting the presented world to one pattern or another, give rise to an impression of a world view, what I shall call a 'mind style'.

Fowler's concept of mind style combines two problematic dimensions of the novel as text. First he raises the possibility of identifying a stylistic property which runs through all levels of the novel. Secondly he claims that the cumulative effect of this will enable us to treat the novel as the embodiment of the opinions and affiliations of its author: in terms of Chatman's diagram we move outward from the centre to the margins; in terms of Leech and Short's we distil a message from the combination of text and discourse. In short, Fowler draws together as a single stylistic principle all of the techniques described above.

It is not too difficult to identify a consistent stylistic signature in the narrative passages of some novels. A classic case is Henry James's tendency to specify a topic (person, situation or idea) by building around it a complex network of modifying and post-modifying clauses. James's sentences attempt consistently to contain and incorporate the multifaceted condition of their subject:

> Yet he was unwilling to take leave, treating his engagement as settled, without some more conventional glance in that direction than he could find an opening for in the manner of the large affable lady who sat there drawing a pair of soiled *gants de Suède* through a fat, jewelled hand and, at once pressing and gliding, repeated over and over everything but the thing he would have liked to hear.
>
> (*The Pupil*, opening passage)

James's complicated system of main and sub-clauses is an attempt to draw together what might otherwise be separate processes of internal and external focalization. In a single sentence he tells us what 'he' is thinking, why he is reluctant to leave the room, and of the physical size, activities, disposition, posture and jewellery of the person who detains him. We might thus argue that the Jamesian mind style involves the omniscient, intradiegetic narrator not only as the controller of the overall narrative structure, but also as someone who strives to synthesize multidimensional experience at a localized stylistic level. We might further argue that since this is a consistent feature of his novels it enables us to move from narrator to implied and real author and infer that this mind style tells us something about the 'world view' of Henry James.

Such procedures are valid in some cases, but not all. As we have seen, some novels can divide the process of focalization between different levels of style and narrative and consequently disrupt any comfortable movement from narrator to real author.

SPEECH, DIALOGUE AND NARRATIVE

The use of dialogue and reported speech can provide an intrusive counterpoint to the stylistic features of the individual narrator.

Leech and Short (1981) and McHale (1978) offer a typology of relations between narrative discourse, speech and conversation.

The two most frequently used methods of differentiating speech from narrative discourse are direct and indirect speech (DS and IS).

> DS: She said, 'I'm going home'.
> IS: She said she would go home.

IS relates closely to narrative reports of speech acts (NRSA). The principal difference is that NRSA offers us the meaning of a character's speech while leaving us uncertain about whether the report is a verbatim account of the words used (IS) or the narrator's paraphrase of their message.

> NRSA: She spoke for five minutes. She wanted to go home.

Free direct speech (FDS) is dialogue with the reporting clause (She said) of DS removed. Novels will sometimes include extended passages of FDS, but the use of pure dialogue as a central structural element would effectively turn the novel in a play (Hemingway's *The Killers* is an exceptional instance of this type of genre-crossing).

Free indirect speech (FIS) involves elements of IS and NRSA. One type of FIS has been called the 'dual voice' (Pascal, 1977). This occurs when the markers or deictic features of a narrative report make us suspect that the report incorporates but does not disclose a speech act. In *Northanger Abbey* the narrator describes Catherine's thoughts about the possible departure of Captain Tilney:

> But Captain Tilney had at present no intention of removing; he was not to be of the party to Northanger, he was to continue at Bath.
>
> (Chapter 19)

Catherine is the focalizer; her thoughts and her perceptions of space and time are the subject of the discourse. One part of the dual voice is the narrator's. The other, we suspect, is a recollection of a speech by Captain Tilney. A more economical way of saying the same thing would be: Captain Tilney would not be going to Northanger; he would be staying in Bath. But the narrator's use of a main clause and two sub-clauses suggests that Catherine's thoughts are constructed from specific exchanges with Captain Tilney: change the tense to the present and insert the personal pronoun and the passage reads rather like Captain Tilney's part in a dialogue regarding his future plans.

As a model for recorded speech FIS has presented a number of problems for linguists and literary critics. In the sentence from *Northanger Abbey* the speech act, if it existed at all, is reconstituted as a discourse controlled by the narrator and focalized as the mental operations of Catherine. It could just as easily satisfy the criteria for Leech and Short's concept of free indirect thought (FIT). A classic case of FIT is the modern technique of interior monologue:

> . . . I near lost my breath yes he said I was a flower of the mountain yes so we are flowers all a womans body yes that was the one true thing he said in his life . . .
>
> (James Joyce, *Ulysses*, 1922: final chapter)

This sequence of unpunctuated, deviant syntax is meant to represent the thought patterns of Molly Bloom at a time when her mind is relaxed and least concerned with immediate practical or ratiocinative operations. She is in bed but not quite asleep. Stylistically it is very different from the *Northanger Abbey* passage, but both involve the reconstitution of recollected speech as part of a single discourse. More significantly, neither discourse is likely to be permissible or necessary outside the genre-specific conventions of the novel. A narrator who knows everything about the thoughts, movements, habits and affiliations of Catherine but who never features in the report of her life is implausible in the real world. Equally implausible is Molly Bloom's long interior monologue. It is unlikely that someone in such a relaxed state of mind could at the same time record her thoughts. If the record were retrospective we have problems with reconciling the detail of the discourse with its impression of immediacy and discontinuity: if her mental operations shifted so rapidly from one deictic focus to another, how could a written record of those patently discontinuous events be either possible or authentic?

Our problem with the passages from *Northanger Abbey* and *Ulysses* lies in our attempts to locate a point of origin for the various strata of reported speech and narrative discourse. Molly Bloom's unstructured thought patterns might be realistic in that they prompt memories of how our own minds function when we are neither fully awake nor asleep. They are unrealistic when we submit them to the practical, circumstantial conditions of writing, composition, recollection and creativity. Similarly the picture of Catherine Morland that emerges from the detailed consideration of her thoughts, motives, ambitions and acts could well correspond with our perception of people in the real world, but unreality intervenes when we begin to ask questions about who imparts this information and how they are able to do it. This sense of tension between the real and the patently unreal dimensions of the text holds the key to any general formula for a stylistics of fiction. As Genette demonstrates, Plato's distinction between diegesis (narrative) and mimesis (imitation, primarily recorded speech) must be qualified by an awareness that the former will always interfere with the latter. And here we find both similarities and distinctions between the stylistics of fiction and the poetic double pattern. In both instances we make sense of the text by balancing the routine non-literary field of interpretation against those elements of the text which disrupt parallels between language and its imagined context. They are different in that while the poetic double pattern tends to inform the localities of language throughout the poem, the novel is often assembled from substantial units of discourse which might of themselves occur in non-literary writing or speech. In the novel the tension between the two halves of the double pattern becomes most evident when we broaden our interpretive framework from a specific passage and seek out a borderline between the refractory conventions of the text and the discourses of the non-fictional world. Epistemological questions such as how Jane Austen's narrator can know so much about the events described without apparently witnessing them, or whether Stephen Dedalus's story is told by a third-person version of himself or by someone else are valid only if we follow the interpretive thread from language to the terms and conditions of the real world. In fiction they become invalid when we recognize that the narrator, the organizing presence of the novel, is actually one element of the self-referring fabric of the text.

Focalization and the different levels of reported speech offer us methods of measuring degrees of interference between style and context in brief extracts. Difficulties arise when we attempt to extrapolate localized findings to the border between the novel and the perceived non-fictional world, and I shall use the following example from Chapter 5 of Joyce's *Portrait* to illustrate this.

> Stephen walked on beside his friend, staring gloomily at the foot-path[1].
> – I tried to love God, he said at length[2]. It seems now I failed. It is very difficult. I tried to unite my will with the will of God instant by instant. In that I did not always fail. I could perhaps do that still – [3]
>   Cranly cut him short by asking:
> – Has your mother had a happy life?
> – How do I know? Stephen said.
> – How many children had she?
> – Nine or ten, Stephen answered[4]. Some died[5].

The passage contains a number of reporting clauses ('Stephen said'), but the absence of inverted commas often blurs the distinction between IS, NRSA, FIS and FIT. Sentence 2 involves a reported speech act, but the reporting clause ('he said at length') makes us suspect that this is an edited version of what Stephen actually said. Sentence 3 is unfinished and returns us to the impression that it is reported verbatim. Sentence 4, with its reporting clause, seems to be direct speech, but we can never be certain if sentence 5 'Some died' is an addition to Stephen's spoken answer or an account of his thoughts.

Throughout this passage, and throughout the novel, the balance between the focalizing agent, Stephen, and the focalizer, the narrator, is uncertain. Consider this passage in relation to Leech and Short's diagram (see p. 56). We might position Stephen and Cranly as addresser and addressee, or vice versa. The words of their spoken exchanges are the text and the discourse is their ongoing interaction, the circumstances that underpin each question and answer and the context inhabited by both speakers. However, this model cannot account fully for our understanding of the passage. For one thing, we cannot make a clear distinction between Stephen's spoken account, his thoughts and the narrator's edited or paraphrased version of these. How can we specify the message encoded by Stephen and decoded by Cranly if we are not certain of the exact nature of the words exchanged?

We could shift the centre of focalization and position the narrator as addresser and ourselves as addressee. The text becomes the entire passage and the discourse incorporates the conventions and techniques by which the narrator encodes the message of the novel and through which we decode it (principally the narrator's third-person account of the acts, experiences, speech and thoughts of Stephen). Sentence 1 offers a compact example of this: the narrator combines an awareness of the activities of Stephen and his friend, their physical location and the mood that underpins Stephen's stare. But we still remain uncertain about the exact position of the narrative focus: is it inside or outside the mind of Stephen?

So far we have treated the passage in much the same way that we would treat non-fictional language: we gradually move outward from the localized style of the text to the controlling presence who narrates it. We attempt to explain the uncertain relation between text, discourse and message by seeking out an overarching source or context. If, in non-fictional discourse, we fail to fully understand the words of the text our next recourse will be to seek further clarification from its initiator or from a broader knowledge of the circumstances which prompted the initiator to create the text. In the novel, however, the model that sustains the interpretive channels of non-fictional discourse will eventually break down. Our knowledge of who the narrator is and of how or why he/she creates specific effects will be provided principally by clues and stylistic patterns within the text, and not by the vast fund of information, linguistic and non-linguistic, which attends actual reports of actual situations and speech acts. The narrator, paradoxically but irrevocably, is an element of his/her own narrative.

5

CONTEXTUALIST STYLISTICS

The theories discussed so far share a common assumption: that the stylistic character of a literary text defines it as literature and distinguishes it from the linguistic rules and conventions of non-literary discourse. The theories are textualist in that they perceive the literary text as a cohesive unity of patterns, structures and effects. Textualists record the ways in which literature borrows features from non-literary language but maintain that these borrowings are transformed by the literary stylistics of the text.

Contextualist stylistics is a broad church, and its various factions are united in their emphasis on the ways in which literary style is formed and influenced by its contexts. These involve (1) the competence and disposition of the reader; (2) the prevailing sociocultural forces that dominate all linguistic discourses, including literature; and (3) the systems of signification through which we process and interpret all phenomena, linguistic and non-linguistic, literary and non-literary.

We will begin with the third of these categories and its influential theorist, Roland Barthes.

BARTHES AND STRUCTURALISM

Roland Barthes's work in semiology (the theory of signs) and structuralism (the systems which govern the operation of signs) has genealogical roots in the work of Saussure and Jakobson. Saussure argued that the structures of language affect and influence our perceptions of reality. In short, the differences and relationships between words can determine rather than simply reflect our perceived distinctions between things and between ideas. Jakobson adapted this thesis to his work on how the structures of poetic language can distort and restructure the refractory indexes of ordinary language. Barthes took both theses a stage further and proposed that we inhabit a network of different sign systems, all of which are capable of creating different levels of interaction between representation and perceived reality, while they themselves share fundamental, interchangeable systems of signification, or grammars.

His most famous comparison between codes of signification involves fashion (clothes) and literature (see *Elements of Semiology*, 1964 and *Système de la mode*, 1967). For example, the manner in which items of clothing are associated with the distinctive elements of the human physique – primarily head, trunk, legs and feet – is comparable with the syntagmatic chain of the sentence; and the choices made at each stage in dressing – shirt or pullover, hat or hood, shoes or trainers – are comparable to the selective possibilities offered by each paradigmatic class of nouns, connectives or adjectives. Barthes's main point is that the conventions which prompt us to choose this or that style of garment are comparable with the conventions that govern our choice of words in the formation of a sentence: both are grounded in the assumption that the sequence of signs includes both an expressive gesture and a concession to the system of signification that makes such a gesture possible. Just as a striking metaphor reflects the writer's skill with the linguistic system as much as his/her original conception of the world, so the 'meaning' of a fashion statement is effectively a function of the conventions of dress that it disrupts.

In *Système* Barthes analyses a number of clothes advertisements, such as 'Dresses are becoming longer; black mink asserts itself.' He argues that such statements are underpinned by an implied assumption that the sign (long dress, black mink) satisfies and reflects broader norms and trends; that by wearing a long dress and black mink we are making a relevant statement. But, argues Barthes, by analysing the systemic codes through which fashion promotes its relevance we can disclose that the codes are arbitrary and related only to meaning by virtue of our willingness to participate in their deceptions.

> Fashion thus becomes an exemplary form of the act of signifi-
> cation and in this way unites with the essence of literature, which
> is to make one read the signifying of things rather than their
> meaning.
>
> (Barthes, 1967: 287)

Barthes's comparison of fashion with literature unsettles textualist stylistics in a number of ways. Textualists frequently base their analysis on the assumption that literary style draws upon elements of non-literary discourses and fictionalizes and/or versifies their previous grounding in the direct communication of meaning. Barthes argues that all codes of meaning and action – literature, fashion, politics, philosophy, eating – involve arbitrary systems of signification. Literature, he contends, is regarded as different only because it is honest about its arbitrary, systematic character; but outside literature 'men deploy an equal energy in masking the systematic nature of their creations and reconverting the semantic relation into a natural or rational one' (1967: 285).

Textualist stylistics, and its predecessor, rhetoric, assume that style, especially literary style, involves a deliberate shift of language away from its pragmatic, functional role of disclosing meaning and towards a zone of playful self-reference. Barthes contends that this notion of style as an arbitrary self-referring system is a condition of all types of discourse.

Barthes's use of the formulae of linguistics and structuralism to analyse a variety of sign systems was not in itself a pioneering strategy. Claude Lévi-Strauss had adapted to his studies in anthropology Jakobson's early work on how the fundamental sound patterns of language (its phonemic features) provide the first step in our ability to distinguish between words and objects. Just as Jakobson's isolation of fifteen universal phonemic features provides the common basis for different morphological and syntactic patterns, so in Lévi-Strauss's schema a similar opposition of primary distinctions underpins the various types of social, familial, sexual, political and ritualistic conventions that constitute each human society or ethnic group (see Bradford, 1994: 118–20).

Barthes's *Writing Degree Zero* (1952; English trans. 1968) predates his more complex structuralist and poststructuralist enterprises. It is his most conventional literary-critical work and in it we find echoes and transmutations of Formalism. His principal objective is to overturn the orthodox distinction between 'style' (predicated upon rhetoric and involving self-consciously literary devices) and 'language' (involving the functional use of signs as an instrument of exchange). He invents the third category of 'writing' (in French, *écriture*) which is the act of creating the text, a point at which the writer negotiates an interface between style and language – and here the Formalist heritage becomes apparent. Style is historically indeterminate. It can develop through time in its acquisition of new modes and devices, but no fictional or poetic style is anchored to a particular historical context. Language, however, is an historical phenomenon: it is at any point imbued with the habits and conventions, and indeed the ideology, of its period. Writing, argues Barthes, involves the interaction of these two elements: 'it is the relationship between creation and society, the literary language transformed by its social finality, form considered as human intention and thus linked to the great crises of History' (1968: 14). What he means by this becomes apparent later in the book. Flaubert, he points out, is a self-consciously literary stylist: 'he builds his narrative by a succession of essences, and not at all by following a phenomenological order [in Shklovsky's model the *sjuzet* envelopes the *fabula*] . . .in the manner of an art drawing attention to its very artificiality' (ibid.: 64–5). However, argues Barthes, Flaubert foregrounds style for a reason. The arbitrary 'Laws' which govern his text correspond with, but by no means replace, the strict conventions of bourgeois society. The 'bourgeois necessity which characterises Frédéric Moreau, Emma Bovary, Bouvard and Pécuchet, requires . . . an art which is equally the bearer of a necessity, and armed with a "Law"' (ibid.: 64). Flaubert's 'writing' on the one hand transcends the historically determined 'language' inhabited by the real life counterpart of Emma Bovary's world, and on the other recreates its deterministic pressures in the 'style' through which her story is mediated.

Barthes, in *Writing Degree Zero* is particularly concerned with the stylistic condition of contemporary, postmodernist literature. The contemporary writer 'is forced by his writing into a cleft stick'. The writer either uses literary style to virtually obliterate the contextual element of the act of creation; or he reproduces the 'vast novelty' of the contemporary world in styles drawn from non-literary discourses. Barthes cites Stéphane Mallarmé's 'typographical agraphia' (visual poems which reduce language to a reflexive emphasis on the material sign) as an example of the former: 'The word . . . is freed from responsibility in relation to all possible context' (ibid.: 75); and Albert Camus's *Outsider* as a case of the latter: 'an ideal absence of style . . . thought remains wholly responsible, without being overlaid by a secondary commitment to form' (ibid.: 77). Barthes diagnoses this modern condition as something that will precipitate a 'zero element' of writing, a kind of pure literature in which the stylistic and the functional states of language will be in a constant, dynamic relationship, without parity or dominance.

Whatever one's opinion on Barthes's presentation of twentieth-century literature, his debt to Formalist theory and Saussurean linguistics is clear enough. The latter proposes that language informs and shapes reality just as much as it reflects it. The former regards the technical distinction between literary and non-literary forms (in Barthes, 'style' and 'language') as a token of the degrees to which language predetermines our modes of thought and perception. The difference between Barthes and his predecessors exists in his refusal to allow the discourse through which we document and comment upon style and language to remain aloof from their shifting dynamic states. As we shall see, in later works such as *S/Z* (1970) he closes the gap between writing about style and the experience and production of style. He breaks down the distinction between literary writing and critical commentary or exegesis: his critical 'writing' enters an interactive, dialogic relationship with the subject text.

READER-RESPONSE AND STYLISTICS

While Jakobson, Lévi-Strauss and other theorists compared the stylistic structures of literature with other social and linguistic systems of organizing meaning, Barthes raised a more fundamental issue: if all systems of language and signification are arbitrary self-referring codes, then so is the system that enables theorists to discuss and document them. In 'The Death of the Author' (1968, in Lodge, 1988) Barthes contends that the multiplicity of stylistic levels, registers and frames of reference that make up a text are focused on 'the reader, not as was hitherto said, the author'. He does not claim that the reader invents the text; rather that the structures that enable us to discuss how its style affects its meaning are part of an *a priori* system of expectations that we impose upon it.

The critic who has done most to pursue the implications for stylistics of reader-centred theory is Stanley Fish. In *Is There a Text in this Class? The Authority of Interpretive Communities* (1980) Fish introduces the concept of literary competence, which is an adaptation of Noam Chomsky's notion of linguistic competence. We acquire linguistic competence as much by habit and experience as by the intensive study of grammar. We listen to linguistic formations used by our parents and peers and, without necessarily being able to reduce these to abstract rules, we implement them in our own manner of communication. Obviously our accent and habits of phrasing will reflect the community in which we acquired linguistic competence, disclosing features such as class, race and region. In Fish's model of literary competence a similar network of influences operates in what he calls the 'interpretive community' of the education system, involving the standard conventions of naming the parts of literary texts and employing them in our analyses and interpretations. Consequently, argues Fish, our perceptions of the stylistic character of literature are due as much to our acquired grammar of interpretation as they are to features that are empirically present within texts.

> Interpretive communities are made up of those who share interpretive strategies not for reading (in the conventional sense) but for writing texts, for constituting their properties and assigning their intentions. In other words, these strategies exist prior to the act of reading and therefore determine the shape of what is read rather than, as is usually assumed, the other way around.
>
> (1980: 171)

For example, the interpretive community equips us with a grammar and vocabulary of interpretation to deal with the local stylistic effects of poetry. Let us return to the opening lines of Milton's *Paradise Lost*:

Of man's first disobedience, and the fruit
Of that forbidden tree, whose mortal taste
Brought death into the world . . .

The interpretive community teaches us that the break between the first and second lines is called enjambment. Our experience of how critics deal with enjambment will encourage us to expect the production of a double meaning; and indeed the line break at 'fruit' does seem to suggest a momentary hesitation between literal meaning (the actual fruit of the tree) and the eventual disclosure of its figurative usage (the fruit or consequence of eating the fruit which 'brought death into the world'). Fish claims, in relation to a similar effect in Milton's *Lycidas*, that 'line endings exist by virtue of perceptual strategies rather than the other way around. Historically, the strategy that we know as "reading (or hearing) poetry" has included paying attention to the line as a unit, but it is precisely that attention that has made the line as a unit . . . available' (1980: 165–6). A textualist critic might argue that Milton's lines do exist, that the iambic pentameter is a verifiable phenomenon. Fish would reply that while we might recognize the presence of linguistic phenomena, our account of how these produce effects is based not upon empirical evidence but upon acquired habits of interpretation.

In 1970 two texts were published which reflect the differences between textualist stylistics and its contextualist, reader-centred counterpart. Jakobson and Jones produced what has become an archetype of Formalist analysis in their dissection of Shakespeare's sonnet 129 (see Jakobson, 1980). In this they document in Shakespeare's poem every instance of what Levin calls coupling. They examine how the quatrains and stanzas of the sonnet variously enclose and underpin its binary themes (life/death, heaven/hell, body/spirit) and how its metre and sound patterns create extra-syntactic parallelisms between practically every word of the text. Barthes in *S/Z* employs a similarly exhaustive stylistic programme in his analysis of Balzac's novella *Sarrasine*. He divides the text into 561 lexies, irreducible units of prose structure, comparable with Jakobson's notion of the phoneme and syllable as the basis for metre and sound pattern. Barthes then examines how the lexies are combined in Balzac's text to produce five levels of effect and response, which he categorizes as the hermeneutic, semic, symbolic, proairetic and cultural codes. These codes are comparable with Jakobson's tracing of relationships between the metrical, syntactic, phonemic, morphological and referential features of the sonnet.

These similarities of method are misleading, because Barthes's work is effectively a parody of Jakobson's. Barthes's 561 lexies can comprise anything from a single word to a series of sentences. He virtually invites the reader to question these classifications, perhaps to consider alternatives. Barthes, tongue firmly in cheek, justifies his division into lexies by claiming that each lexie foregrounds a particular engagement with one or more of his five codes. At the same time his own use of these codes brings their validity into question. Frequently he digresses upon the kind of reader who would be especially interested in the operation of particular codes. Digression number LXXI focuses upon lexie 414 in which Sarrasine embraces a castrato in the mistaken belief that he is a woman. Barthes acknowledges that the code in operation here will depend upon the disposition of the reader: one reader might emphasize the proairetic (narrative) code and be interested in what happens next; another might give most attention to the cultural code, particularly in relation to his/her own experiences of sexuality and its cultural formations.

Barthes's *S/Z* is a demonstration of his thesis that the stylistic patterns and effects of texts are non-empirical, in a constant state of formation and change according to the circumstances of interpretation and the condition of the reader.

A more straight-faced critique of Jakobsonian, textualist stylistics is found in Jonathan Culler's *Structuralist Poetics* (1975: 55–75) where Culler applies the formulae of coupling and parallelism that Jakobson had used on Shakespeare's sonnet to an extract from Jakobson's critical prose. Culler's exercise is convincing and persuasive, and he claims that linguistics 'does not solve the problem of what constitutes a pattern and hence does not provide a method for the discovery of patterns. *A fortiori*, it does not provide a procedure for the discovery of poetic patterns' (1975: 65). The validity of Culler's claim can only properly be discussed after a careful reading of his book and of the work of Fish, Jakobson and Barthes, but the relatively uninformed and undecided reader will notice an obvious flaw in his thesis. It is certainly the case that Jakobson's methods of stylistic analysis are founded upon developments in linguistics that have occurred beyond and outside the production of its literary subjects. But surely Culler cannot question the actuality of a text consisting of fourteen iambic lines and divided into three rhymed quatrains and a couplet. The sonnet must 'constitute a pattern' which is far more common in poetry than it is in everyday conversation, or in discursive prose. It does not require a 'procedure' for its 'discovery'; it exists. This quarrel between textualist and contextualist stylistics will be covered in more detail in Chapter 13, on evaluative stylistics.

SOCIOLINGUISTICS

Sociolinguistics is an umbrella term covering a variety of methods and objectives, but there is a close relationship between the approaches to literary style adopted by reader response theorists and sociolinguists. Roger Fowler, one of the latter group's most eminent spokesmen, comments on Jakobson: 'I think it is clear that Jakobson's concentration on formal structure is determined not by the nature of the material but by his decision to treat it in such a way' (1981: 84). Jakobson's decision, argues Fowler, promotes a cultural ideal of literature as a 'contained, quiet, socially un-responsive object outside of history' (ibid.: 85). Fowler promotes a sociolinguistic programme for the study of literary style.

> [B]asically it is theory of varieties, of correlations between distinctive linguistic choices and particular socio-cultural circumstances. The individual text can be described and interpreted in relation to the

stylistic conventions which generate it and the historical and socio-logical situation which brought it into existence.

(ibid.: 174)

Fowler's programme differs from Jakobson's in that whereas the latter held that there is a 'split' between the figures and stylistic elements of the text and the world outside the text, the former argues that the linguistic conventions and habits of the world – involving ideological and social registers – influence and permeate the stylistic character of the text.

The figure who effectively invented this method of socio-linguistic study was Mikhail Bakhtin, a theorist who drew upon yet transformed the methods of Formalism. Bakhtin has this to say on the language of the novel:

> The author participates in the novel (he is omnipresent in it) with *almost no direct language of his own.* The language of the novel is a *system* of languages that mutually and ideologically interanimate each other. It is impossible to describe and analyze it as a single unitary language.
>
> (1967; repr. in Lodge, 1988: 130)

The novel borrows liberally from a variety of non-literary discourses – reported speech, free association monologues, letters, journals, non-fictional accounts of places and objects – and the emphasis of much criticism is upon the ways in which these elements are unified in a single text or subordinated to a domi-nant narrative structure. Bakhtin shifts the emphasis towards the relationship between the competing discourses of the text and their origins outside the text:

> To a greater or lesser extent, every novel is a dialogical system made up of the images of 'languages', styles and consciousnesses that are concrete and inseparable from language. Language in the novel not only represents, but itself serves as the object of representation. Novelistic discourse is always criticizing itself.
>
> (ibid.: 131)

This is a brief account of Bakhtin's now famous concept of dialogism: there is a competitive 'dialogue' between the various styles in the text, supplemented by the text's attempt to alter and reshape the discourses it has borrowed from the non-fictional world. This model of fiction corresponds with Fowler's objective of investigating the style of the text in relation to the 'historical and sociological situation which brought it into existence'.

In Elizabeth Gaskell's novel *North and South* (1854) an anonymous third-person narrator describes encounters between Margaret Hale, a well-spoken New Forest parson's daughter, and the inhabitants of Darkshire in the industrial North. Here, she visits Nicholas Higgins, mill worker, who

> seemed, by his manners, to have entered a little more on the way of humility; he was quieter, and less self-asserting.
>
> 'So th'oud gentleman's away on his travels, is he?' said he. 'Little 'uns told me so . . .'.
>
> 'Is that the reason you're so soon at home tonight?' asked Margaret innocently.

(Chapter 41)

It is generally agreed, given Gaskell's own educated middle-class origins and affiliations, that her novel is an objective, dispassionate account of the social tensions and injustices of Victorian England. However, the stylistic tensions of the novel itself question this judgement.

As with Jane Austen's Catherine and her extradiegetic narrator, Margaret Hale's thoughts and actions dominate the narrative while the narrator occasionally exercises a degree of omniscience in his/her ability to record the non-verbal moods and thoughts of other characters. But it is noticeable that characters such as Higgins are described only in terms of external focalization. We listen to them, we know what they want, and why they do what they do, but their mental focus never permeates the third-person narrative.

It would be simplistic to regard this as a case of class-conscious elitism, and Bakhtin provides a more subtle analytical model.

> [T]here is no unitary language or style in the novel. But at the same time there does exist a centre of language (a verbal-ideological centre) for the novel. The author (as creator of the novelistic whole) cannot be found at any one of the novel's language levels: he is to be found at the centre of organization where all levels intersect.
>
> (Lodge, 1988: 131)

Imagine what would happen if Gaskell's narrator were to move from Higgins's reported speech to an account of the ideas and emotions that underpin it. There would be a bizarre contrast between the narrator's own stylistic signature (closely resembling Margaret's mode of address) and Higgins's dialect. The thoughts and words of the same character would occupy two very different stylistic registers. Moreover, what Bakhtin calls 'the centre of organization where all levels intersect' would be disrupted. The contrast would unsettle the stylistic and indeed the social complicity between principal character, narrator and author.

In his essay on 'Anti-language in Fiction' (1981: 142–61) Fowler draws upon Bakhtin's concept of dialogism (focused mainly on the nineteenth-century novel) and examines the way in which two modern novels, Anthony Burgess's *A Clockwork Orange* (1962) and William Burroughs's *The Naked Lunch* (1959), reposition subversive, subcultural forms of slang and dialect at the centre of the text. 'The question is whether the author is prepared to allow his working class characters any kind of free identity, freedom to challenge or even invent the middle class norms [as do Burgess and Burroughs], or whether their values are submerged, neutralized by middle class ideology [as in Gaskell and most other nineteenth-century novels]' (Fowler, 1981: 158).

Sociolinguistics differs from its textualist counterparts in that it seeks to find causal relationships between the stylistic character of literary texts and their social and ideological contexts. Easthope's

Poetry as Discourse (1983) follows the traditional chronology of literary history, and acknowledges the stylistic differences between Augustan, Romantic and modernist poems. But it discusses these differences not as purely aesthetic alterations, but in terms of the notion of 'discourse'. Discourse in this sense refers to a collection, at a specific time in history, of different stylistic registers with different purposes (political, literary, social) which transmit and maintain institutionalized values or ideologies. This model of discourse derives principally from the work of Michel Foucault (see *The Order of Things*, 1970). Saussure proposed that the relation between the linguistic system and the continuum of objects, events and ideas that it represents is arbitrary, that the structures of language enable us to discriminate between concepts and ideas. Foucault extended this thesis to our perceptions of history and ideology, arguing that the various discourses of a period and society promote and institutionalize its fears, hatreds, obsessions and ideals. Foucault's ideas have affected literary stylistics in that they underpin a branch of criticism known as new historicism.

FEMINIST STYLISTICS

Feminist stylistics shares with new historicism a view of discourse as something which transmits social and institutionalized prejudices and ideologies, specifically the respective roles and the mental and behavioural characteristics of men and women. Feminism differs from new historicism in its view that literature, defined by its stylistic character, represents a special instance of the mediation and formation of perceived gender roles. Many of the major issues in contemporary feminist criticism were addressed in Virginia Woolf's *A Room of One's Own* (1929; quotation from reprints in Mary Eagleton, 1986: 7–8, 547–50, 594–6) and stylistics plays a significant part in Woolf's thesis. She argues that the principal pre-twentieth-century women writers became novelists because the 'older forms' (drama and poetry) were 'hardened and set': 'The novel was young enough to be soft in her hands.' The novel offered women writers a flexible network of conventions, one that would be more responsive to the experience of the writer than the monolithic, male-dominated precedents of the 'older' genres. Woolf goes on to claim that Jane Austen and Dorothy Richardson 'invented' syntactic patterns, 'which we might call the psychological sentence of the feminine gender. It is of a more elastic fibre than the old, capable of stretching to the extreme, of suspending the frailest particles, of enveloping the vaguest shapes.' This raises the disturbing question of whether style is a predetermined condition, of whether women write differently because they are women, and finally of whether women who write justify the old chauvinistic axiom that there is a specific and largely predictable state of being and activity generally known as the feminine. Woolf is aware of this, and she shifts the perspective from style to subject: 'the essential difference lies in the fact not that men describe battles and women the birth of children, but that each sex describes itself. The first words in which either a man or a woman is described are generally enough to determine the sex of the writer.' The problematic relation between feminism, style and context uncovered in Woolf's essay lives on in more recent work. Sara Mills in Chapter 1 of *Feminist Stylistics* (1995) conducts a lengthy investigation of the notion of male and female literary styles. She cites Ellen Moers's investigation of the prevalence of metaphors connected with birds (indicating traditionally feminine attributes of delicacy, vulnerability and beauty) in the work of a number of major women writers (Moers, in Mary Eagleton, 1986: 206) and reports an experiment conducted with Strathclyde University undergraduates on what they perceived as character-istically male and female forms of sentence construction. The undergraduates reinforced conventional gender stereotypes by judging aggressive, direct, concise sentences as male and more elaborate, grammatically complex and consequently less purposive sentences as female (see also Cameron's *Feminism and Linguistic Theory*, 1985).

These surveys indicate that the parallels between style and gender have as much to do with the expectations of the reader as with the intrinsic mental, psychological and cultural characteristics of men and women: Mills reprints a sequence from a novel by Iris Murdoch which fully satisfies the criteria for male sentence structure employed by the students. With this in mind let us consider the following extract:

> He heard, but did not notice the click of the door. Suddenly he started. He saw, in the shaft of ruddy, copper-coloured light near him, the face of a woman. It was gleaming like fire, watching him, waiting for him to be aware. It startled him terribly. He thought he was going to faint. All his suppressed, subconscious fear sprang into being, with anguish.
>
> 'Did I startle you?' said Ursula, shaking hands with him. 'I thought you had heard me come in.'
>
> 'No,' he faltered, scarcely able to speak. She laughed, saying she was sorry. He wondered why it amused her.
>
> 'It is so dark,' she said. 'Shall we have the light?'
>
> And moving aside she switched on the strong electric lights. The classroom was distinct and hard, a strange place after the soft dim magic that filled it before she came. Ursula turned curiously to look at Birkin. His eyes were round and wondering, bewildered, his mouth quivered slightly. He looked like one who is suddenly wakened.

The passage is from Chapter 3 of D. H. Lawrence's *Women in Love* (1921). I have altered it by switching the gender of the pronouns and reversing the positions of the proper names, Birkin and Ursula. The result is that Ursula becomes the dominant presence. She is responsible for the physical acts – particularly the click of the door and the electric light – that cause the rather feeble Birkin to become faint and bewildered. She does the watching; he is watched. Most readers will find the effects of the revised text rather unusual, even more so for a novel published in 1921. Our initial reaction would be that the novel is self-consciously a woman's text, a strident promotion of the female character as someone who, without necessarily threatening her male partner, imposes her presence upon the narrative structure that they both inhabit.

Now let us test these impressions against an analysis of the original text:

> 'Did I startle you?' said Birkin, shaking hands with her.
>
> 'I thought you had heard me come in.'
>
> 'No,' she faltered, scarcely able to speak. He laughed, saying he was sorry. She wondered why it amused him.
>
> 'It is so dark,' he said. 'Shall we have the light?'
>
> And moving aside he switched on the strong electric lights. The classroom was distinct and hard, a strange place after the soft dim magic that filled it before he came. Birkin turned curiously to look at Ursula. Her eyes were round and wondering, bewildered, her mouth quivered slightly. She looked like one who was suddenly awakened.

In purely technical terms the narrator is extradiegetic. He/she maintains an apparent level of omniscient objectivity by shifting the centre of focalization between setting, reported speech and the private thoughts of both characters. However, there is a patent collusion between the described activities of the original male character and the apparent impartiality of the narrator. The electric light is 'strong'; it suffuses the room with an atmosphere that is 'distinct and hard', in contrast with the 'soft dim magic' felt when the (originally female) character was alone. In the original the narrator appears to collate specific purposive acts (opening the door, switching on the light) with effects and moods that are characteristically male. But we only really notice this relation between gender stereotype and description when the roles are altered, when it is the woman who occupies the active position in the narrative. This is comparable with the likely effect upon the Strathclyde undergraduate of an encounter with a woman who habitually uses the clipped, aggressive syntactic structures that the undergraduate associates with maleness.

Let us now turn back to Leech and Short's diagram on p. 56. In this they offer two different tracks between addresser and addressee: one through the text, the other through a more complex network of discourses that affect the way the text is written and read. By altering the pronouns in this extract I have attempted to show the interdependent relation between these two tracks. The altered 'female' text is more unusual, unexpected than the original not because the style is experimental or different from other novels we have read. It is odd because the mental image it creates is different from the predominant conventions of male–female activities offered by discourses outside the text.

A more detailed survey of the interactions of style, gender, writer, reader and literary history will be offered in Part III, Chapter 12: 'Gender and Genre'.

FUNCTIONAL STYLISTICS

The term 'functional stylistics' accounts for the uneasy, almost para-doxical, relationship between a number of linguistic theories of the 1950s and 1960s and their use in literary stylistics. These theories are for the most part functional, in that they focus on the ways in which the linguistic system operates in terms of its utilitarian functions. We choose this or that word or syntactic formation according to the requirements of the context of their use and as a result of our desire to achieve an effective, functional, transference of meaning. The use of these theories as a model for literary-stylistic analysis is paradoxical because the context of, say, a real conversa-tion is grounded in our knowledge of its actual circumstances whereas in a novel its context would be comprised of the stylistic keys and registers that constitute the fabric of the text.

Noam Chomsky is probably the most influential figure in functional linguistics. In *Syntactic Structures* (1957) he devised the model for transformational-generative grammar, in which every linguistic construction is seen as 'consisting of' other component constructions. For instance the sentence

The men were playing the game

would be represented as a sequence of NP (Noun Phrase – the men) and VP (Verb Phrase – were playing the game). At a localized level the VP consists of V + NP, and the NP consists of Art (article 'the') + N. The same sentence could be 'transformed' from its active to its passive form, 'The game was played by the men', and the elements of 'phrase structure grammar' described above would be employed to show how the transformation takes place.

Chomsky's system of 'phrase structure grammar' begs a number of questions; most significantly how and why do individual speakers choose an active rather than a passive version of the above sentence, or vice versa? Chomsky answered (1965) with the thesis that 'linguistic competence' is what makes 'linguistic performance' possible. Linguistic competence is the internalized blueprint ('the deep structure') that enables the speaker to produce the statement ('the surface structure'). The two sentences quoted above are surface manifestations of the same deep structure. Their difference can be explained in terms of their user's decision to emphasize the importance of either the game or the players in his/her description of a particular event, combined with his/her acquired ability to redistribute a particular group of nouns, verbs and articles.

Chomsky's formula has been applied in literary stylistics in a number of ways, with varying degrees of success. In 'Generative Grammars and the Concept of Literary Style' (Ohmann 1970. See also Thorne, 1965) Richard Ohmann attempted to 'clear away a good deal of the mist from stylistic theory' (1970: 263) by isolating the original deep structures from which writers derive their individual stylistic signatures. For example, the following is a sentence from Ernest Hemingway's story 'Soldier's Home':

> So his mother prayed for him and then they stood up and Krebs kissed
> his mother and went out of the house.

Ohmann reduces this sentence to its fundamental phrase structure
units – its deep structure:

> So his mother prayed for him. Then they stood up and Krebs kissed
> his mother. Krebs went out of the house.

Ohmann notes that the 'reduced passage still sounds very much
like Hemingway' and he compares this case of reduction to deep
structures with what happens when the same procedure is applied
to passages of third-person prose from novels by William Faulkner
and Henry James. In both instances there is a far more complex
sequence of transformations from the reduced units of deep structure to Faulkner's stream of consciousness and James's byzantine
complexities of sentence structure than would appear to divide
the deep from the surface structures of Hemingway's prose.

There are a number of problems with this procedure (some
of which are raised by McLain, 1976). Ohmann's reduction of
Hemingway's stark prose, Faulkner's stream of consciousness technique and James's network of main and sub-clauses to virtually
identical principles of deep structure makes the assumption that
writing novels, like engaging in conversation, begins with an
irreducible message or impression. As shown earlier, the construction of a third-person narrative involves levels of focalization
and identification with the thoughts of different characters. The
attendant processes of syntactic generation and transformation are
very different from those employed by a person attempting to
deliver a particular message in a particular situation. The linguistic
competence of novel writing is acquired partly through an awareness of how other novelists have variously shaped and distorted the
registers of ordinary language. In short, Chomsky's notion of deep
and surface structure is based upon an assumption that the
linguistic product will be formed principally by the desire to

deliver effectively the intended message, while fiction writing reverses this relationship: the style of the novel *creates* the message.

A similar tension between the governing principles of non-literary language and those of literary style would emerge if we attempted to employ transformational-generative procedures to poetry. Let us return to the quotation from Donne's 'The Flea', where the speaker states, 'Though parents grudge, and you'. This surface structure is loose and slightly ambiguous, but we cannot simply reduce it to a correct deep structure because to do so would be to project the speaker into a very real situation of hesitant improvised speech. The fact that the poet encloses the surface structure in an iambic pattern reminds us that the speaker and the situation are, just as much as the syntax, the product of the fictive, formalized discourse of poetry.

Chomsky's model of deep and surface structure presented literary stylistics with more questions than answers. By conflating the structure and context of ordinary language it obliged literary linguistics to re-examine the ways in which this relationship operates in the literary text. Ohmann effectively projected narrative style into the field of non-fictional discourse. The contributors to the 1956 *Kenyon Review* symposium on poetic form followed a different track.

Seymour Chatman (1956) proposed for poetic form an analytic technique based upon the identification of two structures. The abstract metrical pattern, such as the iambic pentameter, is the deep structure. The surface structure consists of the variations in stress, pitch and pause permitted by the deep structure. For example, Milton's line

Sūch pléas/uře tóok/the Sérp/eñt tó/bē hóld

maintains an iambic pattern (deep structure) in that the relative stress values of consecutive syllables represent five movements from lower to higher. However, if we were to grade these values according to a broader normative scale of stress values the variations (surface structure) would become more complex. On a simple scale of 1 to 4 the emphasis would be graded as:

2   4   2   3 1   3   1 2 1   3
Such pleas/ure took/the Serp/ent to/be hold

In this grading the unstressed syllable 'ure' carries the same stress value as the stressed syllable 'to'. Overall there is a tension between the abstract deep structure of five unstress–stress units and the more flexible surface structure where the relative stress values maintain a higher emphasis in the first two feet (between 2 and 4) than in the last three (between 1 and 3). Jakobson (1960) calls the deep structure 'verse design' and the surface structure 'verse instance'.

Unlike Ohmann's method, this formula (known as linguistic metrics) does not project poetry into the field of non-poetic discourse. Rather, it foregrounds the ways in which the patterns of non-poetic discourse are operative but contained within the formal structures of poetry. It shows how there can be a counterpoint between the intonational pattern of a sentence which crosses the line ending (surface structure) and the repeated deep structure of the metrical lines themselves. While Ohmann carries the analytical methods of non-literary linguistics into his discussion of literary texts, linguistic metrics maintains that poems appropriate the structural features of non-literary language and adapt them to their formal conventions.

This uneasy relationship between functional linguistics and literary stylistics features also in J. L. Austin's theory of speech acts. Austin (1962) refined the speech act into three categories: (1) the act of uttering (the locutionary act); (2) the act performed in saying something, e.g. promising, swearing, threatening, warning (illocutionary act); and (3) the act performed as a result of saying something, e.g. persuading (perlocutionary act). Within this formula, language and its structural formations function as an element of the conditions which prompt it and its actual consequences. Ohmann, again (1971), discusses how these three levels of the speech act become prominent in drama, where pre-linguistic conditions, acts and consequences underpin the language of the text. He is less confident about the relevance of speech act theory to literary texts, such as novels and poems, where context is effectively a product of stylistic devices and textual formations. He concedes that literature in general should be categorized as a 'quasi-speech act'; that although a literary text can recreate the illocutionary and perlocutionary conditions of a speech act these conditions are themselves dependent upon the broader linguistic fabric of the text.

For example, the opening of Eliot's 'Prufrock' involves an illocutionary prompt to 'Let us go then, you and I'. In real circumstances the locutionary act could be explained in terms of who the 'you and I' are and their proposed destination. In the poem all three circumstantial details become devices upon which Eliot builds a network of supplementary questions, metaphors and sociocultural references, none of which ever comes to rest upon a specific speaker, hearer or proposition. The text absorbs the context (see below pp. 159–62 for a further discussion of 'Prufrock').

CONCLUSION: THE DOUBLE PATTERN

So far I have considered a variety of twentieth-century theories of stylistics. The rest of the book will put these methods and ideas to the test. In Parts II and III I shall make frequent use of the concept of the double pattern, introduced on pp. 46–50. The stylistic features of a poem include devices and registers that bear allegiance both to the formal inheritance of the genre and to those elements which the poem shares with non-poetic discourses: the active relationship between these two poles is the double pattern. Similarly, the novel will organize and situate non-literary modes and registers in a way that is particular to fiction writing: again their relationship involves the double pattern.

The double pattern outside the text reflects the attention given by the interpreter to one or other pole of the double pattern within it. This interpretive divide has already become apparent in the division between textualism and contextualism. A textualist will be concerned principally with the ways in which the patently literary structure of the text appropriates and refracts its references to the world. A contextualist will be more concerned with the text as a constituent feature of a much broader range of discourses and stylistic networks: syntactic, lexical, political, historical, gendered, cultural. The textualist and the contextualist will acknowledge the pressure of the double pattern within the text, but they will differ on the effects and function of literary style. For example, Roland Barthes is a contextualist in that he regards the double pattern as an active relationship between style and function, sign and meaning, that operates in all fields of representation: literature is not unique. Fish is a contextualist in that he regards the double pattern as a structure imposed upon the text by the reader, a pretence sustained by the conventions, habits and expectations of the broader interpretive community. Fowler's vision of the double pattern is that the stylistic, literary pole is a function of social and historical forces: the structure of a text is a condition of its context.

Empson, Brooks and Jakobson are textualists. They perceive the double pattern of poems as a means by which the text appropriates the functional, referential condition of language to the stylistic field of the poem itself. Shklovsky, Genette, Todorov and Chatman regard the double pattern of the novel as a stylistic field in which local non-literary registers (such as dialogue) become part of the architecture of textual interrelations that in the real world are random and contingent.

The stylistic pattern plays a significant role in our perceptions of literary history, the principal subject of Part II. Language is always dependent upon its historical context. The conventions of speaking and writing reflect or engage with the social, political or ideological resonances of a word, a phrase or a locutionary habit, and these non-literary registers inform the texture of poems, plays and novels. At the same time certain elements of literary writing maintain an oblique and sometimes independent relationship with the forces that shape the broader mutations of language. The linguistic habits of Jane Austen's characters and the syntactic and lexical formations of her narrators are firmly rooted in early nineteenth-century English. However, the abstract structure of her novels (the relation between focalizer and focalizing agent; the stylistic joints between narrative and dialogue) recurs throughout nineteenth-century and twentieth-century fiction. The development and endurance of literary style and its engagement with contemporary discourses will be explained differently by textualist and contextualist critics. Neither school can offer a comprehensive account of whether historical circumstances or literary inheritance finally decides the stylistic character of a text. The tension within the text between these two axes, and outside it between stylistic theories, will be the subject of Part II.

PART II

STYLISTICS AND LITERARY HISTORY

6

RENAISSANCE AND AUGUSTAN POETRY

THE RELIC

When my grave is broke up again
Some second guest to entertain,
(For graves have learned that woman-head
To be to more than one a bed)
    And he that digs it, spies
A bracelet of bright hair about the bone,
    Will he not let us alone,
And think that there a loving couple lies,
Who thought that this device might be some way
To make their souls, at the last busy day,
Meet at this grave, and make a little stay?

If this fall in a time, or land,
Where mis-devotion doth command,
Then, he that digs us up, will bring

> Us, to the Bishop, and the King,
>> To make us relics; then
> Thou shalt be a Mary Magdalen, and I
>> A something else thereby;
> All women shall adore us, and some men;
> And since at such time, miracles are sought,
> I would have that age by this paper taught
> What miracles we harmless lovers wrought.
>
> First, we loved well and faithfully,
> Yet knew not what we loved, nor why,
> Difference of sex no more we knew,
> Than our guardian angels do;
>> Coming and going, we
> Perchance might kiss, but not between those meals;
>> Our hands ne'er touched the seals,
> Which nature, injured by late law, sets free:
> These miracles we did; but now alas,
> All measure, and all language, I should pass,
> Should I tell what a miracle she was.

(John Donne, 1633)

What can the various techniques and strategies of modern stylistics tell us about this poem? We will begin by considering what the language of the poem tells us about the speaker, his subject and the context of the utterance. The deictic features of the poem, those which orientate or anchor the utterance to a particular space, time and viewpoint, will play an important part in this process.

The poem is a first-person speculation on what might happen if a gravedigger were to discover the contents of the addresser's coffin. The language in the first two stanzas is dominated by the conditional mood – 'Will he [the gravedigger] not . . . '; 'If this fall . . . '; 'I would have . . . '. In the third stanza this mood is intercut with what appears to be a more certain account of the earlier activities of the addresser and his female partner.

This female functions for much of the poem as the apparent addressee ('Then/Thou shalt be . . . '), but there is evidence to discount this. After the speaker has speculated, fantasized about their memory and (his) remains being treated as religious relics, and has recalled their mortal relationship, he refers to the woman in the past tense, with an indirect pronoun: 'Should I tell what a miracle *she was*'. And why, we wonder, will he be buried with 'a bracelet of [her] bright hair about the bone'? This, he suggests, might make the finder '*think*' 'that there a loving couple lies'. Surely a loving couple would have been buried together? The more we speculate on the circumstances which prompted this peculiar utterance, the more the addresser emerges as a disturbed, traumatized individual. What does he mean at the beginning of the third stanza by 'First, we loved well and faithfully'? What happened after that? It seems that their relationship was in any event a tentative, platonic encounter. Their sexuality was no more evident than that of their asexual 'guardian angels'. Not once did they touch 'the seals/Which nature, injured by late law, sets free'. The suspicion that their unconsummated liaison was a problem for the addresser seems confirmed by the almost obsessive pattern of religious imagery, especially the presentation of her as 'a Mary Magdalen' and himself as 'A something else', presumably Jesus Christ. We might wonder if the images of mortality and sexuality transfigured by spirituality, and consequently guaranteed eternal significance, is a strategy, conscious or subliminal, of self-consolation.

What we are doing is using the language of the text, particularly its deictic features, as a means of reconstructing contextual events and circumstances; we have assembled from the language of the poem a speaking presence with a personal history and an identifiable set of concerns. This procedure can be classified under a heading which I have already used, as linguisic functionalism.

The words of the text or utterance are used as channels to the interpersonal and contextual situation which prompted them. Functionalism focuses less upon 'What do the words mean?' and more upon 'What does the speaker mean by the words?' Speech act theory is a philosophical branch of linguistic functionalism: the functions, intentions, goals and effects of the utterance are its principal focus.

Literary stylistics shifts the centre of attention from the situation of the utterance to the words of the text; more specifically to the degree to which the structure, the style of the text, interferes with or clarifies perceived images of its situation, context and paraphrasable meaning.

The most insistent, pervasive stylistic feature of the poem is its metrical and stanzaic framework. The rhyme scheme is a complex aab bcd dce e e system, overlaid upon a pattern consisting of four octosyllabic lines followed by a six-syllable, a ten-syllable and another six-syllable line and concluded with four pentameters. These variations achieve an effect of spontaneity – metre and rhyme seem to be following the largely informal syntax of speech – but we must also recognize, not least because the stanzaic pattern is repeated with admirable precision, that the 'spontaneity' is a contrived effect.

Already we can consider a tension between the stylistic features of the text and its functional context: the double pattern. Consider line 8 of the second stanza:

All women shall adore us, and some men;

In general linguistic terms the surface structure of this clause is slightly ambiguous: does it mean that all women and some men shall adore us or that we, and some men, will be adored by all women? Common sense tells us that the former is more likely to be the case, and we can reinterpret the surface structure in terms of its deep structure; the syntactic framework which underpins its more ambiguous surface form.

All women and some men shall adore us.

The translation of surface structure into its underlying deep structure is a linguistic procedure which falls under the rules of transformational or generative grammar devised by Chomsky (1965). If the surface structure is ambiguous or grammatically deviant the deep structure enables us to stabilize or clarify its meaning, but of more significance is the question of why a particular surface structure was produced. Functionalists will look for an answer to this in terms of the unknown circumstantial conditions of the utterance. In this instance the slightly ambiguous syntactic slippage is consistent with the general informality of the syntax and with the perceived trauma of the speaking presence. However, stylistics provides us with another perspective on the deep–surface structure relationship. It could be argued that the positioning of the phrase 'and some men' is prompted as much by the need to maintain an iambic pattern and to conform to the rhyme scheme as it is by the spontaneous impropriety of speech. The correct, deep structure would contain the same words but it would disrupt the formal structure of the stanza.

Throughout the poem Donne maintains an interactive relationship between its stylistic and functional registers. The structural centre of the first sentence of stanza 1 is the conditional relation between the two main verb phrases: 'When my grave is broke up . . . . Will he [the digger] not let us alone . . . '. Tied into this are a number of qualifying and digressive sub-clauses on why the grave would be reopened, the figurative relation between this practice and the mortal experience of men and women going to bed, the bracelet of bright hair about the bone and the effect of this upon the gravedigger. The general effect is of someone organizing their thoughts, recollections and hypotheses as speech. The linguistic term for this is embedded syntax. Instead of making his statement in specific, consecutive sentences the speaker embeds related and supplementary information in sub-clauses subordinate to the main sentence. The functionalist would regard this as a consistent feature of spoken, spontaneous language: the speaker will begin a sentence, pause, include a qualifying phrase, move on, specify the context and complete the sentence.

The stylistic features of the text oblige us to revise this hypothesis. It is impossible to imagine a real context in which a distraught speaker could organize his/her speech into the bewilderingly complex, thrice-repeated stanzaic structure of the text. The stylistic structure of the poem operates on two levels: the double pattern. On the one hand there are features that the poem shares with other linguistic genres and discourses (the words are organized into sentences and supply us with basic information about time, place and point of view). On the other, these intrageneric features are organized by a pattern of metre and rhyme that is patently poetic. Compare 'The Relic' with a sonnet by Donne's contemporary, George Herbert.

PRAYER (I)

Prayer the Church's banquet, Angels' age,
    God's breath in man returning to his birth,
    The soul in paraphrase, heart in pilgrimage,
The Christian plummet sounding heaven and earth;
Engine against the Almighty, sinners tower,
    Reversèd thunder, Christ-side-piercing spear
    The six-day's-world transposing in an hour,
A kind of tune, which all things hear and fear;
Softness, and peace, and joy, and love, and bliss,
    Exalted manna, gladness of the best,
    Heaven in ordinary, man well dressed,
The milky way, the bird of paradise,
    Church bells beyond the stars heard, the souls' blood,
    The land of spices; something understood.

This sonnet consists of a single sentence, but it is an incomplete sentence. Its subject is 'Prayer' but this carries no predicate verb.

Instead of stating that 'Prayer is', 'Prayer means' or 'Prayer involves' any of the subsequent catalogue of conditions or activities, Herbert endlessly defers any direct grammatical or causal relation between the subject and its associations. A sentence without a predicate and consisting of clauses without explicit conjunctions is known in rhetoric as asyndetic and falls within the general linguistic concept of parataxis. Parataxis is often hurried, uncertain or indecisive speech in which clauses are linked by juxtaposition rather than explicit grammatical connectives. We make sense of a paratactic utterance by translating the surface structure into its assumed deep structure. The surface structure of 'Liked him, good man' would generally be underpinned by the deep structure: (I) liked him, (because he was a) good man'. However, any attempt to apply the normative procedures of functionalism to Herbert's sonnet brings us up against a problem similar to that raised by 'The Relic'. The only available explanations for sentences without predicates or for deviant paratactic utterances are grounded in the functionalist model of an interdependency of language and context. There is generally a reason for the speaker's deviation from the grammatical norm: illiteracy, dialect, the various states of shock, uncertainty or nervousness brought on by the circumstances of the utterance.

The positioning of this utterance within the structure of the sonnet effectively obstructs any attempt to contextualize it as contingent upon circumstances external to the text. Traditionally the four parts of the sonnet, the three quatrains followed by the concluding couplet, organize and foreground a sequence of epigrams, hypotheses or propositions: as Jakobson has demonstrated, the 'message' of the typical Renaissance sonnet consists of a continuous interaction of syntactic deep structures with metre, sound pattern and rhyme scheme. Herbert's single sentence gives the impression that the addresser is incapable of answering the question posited in the opening noun. 'Prayer' is transposed with practically every human experience, temporal and spiritual, but this accumulative collage never comes to rest upon a predicate verb.

Herbert juxtaposes the enigmatic uncertainty of the syntax with the secure formal architecture of the sonnet form.

In both poems, what Jakobson refers to as the 'split' between the addresser within the text and his imagined counterpart in the real world is constantly foregrounded. Compare these poems with the following extract from Pope's *An Essay on Criticism* (1711):

> 'Tis with our judgments as our watches; none
> Go just alike, yet each believes his own.
> In Poets as true Genius is but rare,
> True Taste as seldom is the Critic's share;
> Both must alike from Heav'n derive their light,
> These born to judge, as well as those to write.
> Let such teach others who themselves excel,
> And censure freely who have written well.
> Authors are partial to their wit, 'tis true,
> But are not Critics to their judgment too?
>
> (lines 9–18)

The relationship between poetic structure and syntax is very different in Pope's poem. In the stanzas of Donne's poem and in Herbert's sonnet, the criss-cross pattern of rhymes which operates as the structural keystone is obliquely related to the consecutive movement of syntax. With Pope's heroic couplets each formal unit is sealed by the aa bb cc rhyme scheme: couplets, like sentences, are consecutive, progressive units of form. These parallels between poetic form and syntax are used by Pope to control and regulate the relation between style and meaning.

Linguistics has devised a number of methods to document the ways in which consecutive sentences create broader patterns of meaning. Textual cohesion, a term coined by Halliday and Hasan in their book *Cohesion in English* (1976), is the tracing of 'ties' between consecutive sentences. Each sentence in a text, following the first, is linked to the content of one or more preceding sentences by at least one tie. A tie is made by some constituent that resumes, restates or reminds us of something designated by a predicate or referring expression in a preceding sentence. Consider the following:

> I like dogs. My whole family likes them. At least, most of them do. We used to have six.

None of these sentences can be fully understood without the others. The 'them' of the second sentence ties into the 'dogs' of the first; 'most of them do' (third) ties into 'my family' (second); 'we' and 'six' tie in, respectively, to 'family' (second and third) and 'dogs' (first and second), and the placing of 'used' creates an intriguing temporal distinction between the fourth sentence and the first three.

Practically all work on the literary-linguistic relevance of cohesion has concentrated on prose; very little emphasis has been placed on how syntactic cohesion is variously disrupted or reinforced by metrical and sound pattern. In Donne's stanzas the ties between the syntactic units maintain a structural pattern that is quite distinct from the formal ties of the rhyme scheme. In Pope's couplets, however, the syntactic and formal ties are carefully co-ordinated. Pope uses the couplet as a kind of supersentence. Each couplet picks up a tie established by one of its predecessors. The theme of literary evaluation as a relative, variable faculty is established in the first couplet. The second couplet, the main clause of a longer sentence, personifies these variables in the figures of the poet and the critic, and the third couplet, the modifying clause, picks up this tie ('Both must . . . '). The fourth couplet, again a complete sentence, relies upon a pre-established theme: 'Let such' would be meaningless without the predicated division between poetical and critical inclinations. The fifth couplet offers a new perspective upon the poet–critic comparison of couplet 2.

In 'The Relic' we constantly encounter a tension between the loose, parenthetic structure of the syntax and the rigid complexities of the form, producing the 'split' between the speaking presence and the controlling hand of the poem. Pope's addresser emerges as a figure whose control of the couplet is just as balanced and purposive as his use of syntax: the couplet becomes an instrument of the addresser rather than a textual structure in which the addresser is enclosed. For example in the first couplet the enjambed break between the pronoun-rhyme word and its verb does not register as a disruption of the balance between poetic form and syntax. Rather, the stylistic effect is deliberate and mimetic: difference in judgement is captured in the metaphor of the watches, and the combined image of uncoordination is mirrored in the structure of the only couplet of the passage in which rhyme scheme and syntax do not 'Go just alike'.

In the second couplet Pope employs the rhetorical device of chiasmus, in which the order of the first phrase is reversed in the second: the words 'poets' and 'critics' occupy precisely opposed positions in their respective metrical and syntactic units, and their respective conditions, 'genius' and 'taste', are similarly, if less exactly, opposed. Pope's control of the balance between the line and syntax operates at two levels. Localized interactions, such as enjambment and chiasmus, are enclosed within individual couplets, while the sequence of couplets is deployed as a supplement to the cohesive progress of separate syntactic units.

In Donne's and Herbert's poems there is a palpable tension between the two elements of the double pattern: features that the poem shares with non-poetic language, particularly syntax, and the patently poetic structure of poetic form. This in turn creates a disjunction between our perceptions of the addresser as an actual figure with concerns and a personal history that lie beyond the text, and the addresser as a construct of the devices and structures deployed by Donne and Herbert. In Pope's poem, syntax and metre are carefully and productively integrated, and addresser and poet are virtually indistinguishable.

Donne's and Herbert's poems belong to a sub-genre of Renaissance lyric verse known as metaphysical poetry. This school of writing flourished between the end of the sixteenth and the mid-seventeenth century. The exploratory, insistent foregrounding of a tension between form and paraphrasable meaning exhibited in both poems is typical of metaphysical style. Pope's poem is an example of Augustan writing, a movement which informed the style of most English verse written between the Restoration of the monarchy in 1660 and the mid-eighteenth century. Augustan poetry takes its name from the Roman Emperor Augustus. Many cultural and political theorists of the late seventeenth and early eighteenth centuries promoted parallels between the relative order and stability of Augustan Rome and the concept of England as a state attempting to build patterns of unity and coherence out of the conflict and instability of the Reformation and the Civil War. Augustan poetry is symptomatic of this broader historical and ideological ideal. In the Renaissance the heroic couplet had been one among many poetic forms and structures. Its ability to enclose referential and metrical structures in brief consecutive units made it an ideal vehicle for satirical verse (and Donne's satires are its most famous pre-Augustan usage). In the Augustan period the couplet became the vehicle for a more comprehensive range of poetic operations – elegies, narratives, love poems, landscape poems. The order and relative predictability which the closed couplet imposes upon the double pattern reflects the appro-priation of Augustan poetry by the much broader political and cultural ideals of its period. Conversely, the range and diversity of Renaissance and metaphysical style – Herbert for example used a different metrical and stanzaic pattern for most of his 140 poems of *The Temple* – could be regarded as symptomatic of the condi-tions that underpinned sixteenth- and early seventeenth-century verse. Just as the political, philosophical and religious norms of the period were subject to continuous change and uncertainty, so its verse created parallel tensions between the two elements of the double pattern.

7

LITERARY STYLE AND LITERARY HISTORY

The stylistic differences between Renaissance and Augustan verse are clear enough and the question of why such a radical change occurred would seem to find ample material for an answer in the social and political background to poetic writing. But the question highlights differences between textualist and contextualist stylistics.

Donald Davie in *Articulate Energy* (1955) divides poetic syntax into five types: subjective, dramatic, objective, like music, like mathematics. Renaissance poetry involves permutations of all five, combined with an equally varied selection of metrical and stanzaic patterns. The Augustan closed couplet reconciled the objective type of syntax with an equally cohesive poetic form: 'it follows a form of action, a movement not through the mind but in the world at large' (Davie, 1955: 79). While the Renaissance lyric replicates the uncertain relation between thought and action in its tensions between the two dimensions of the double pattern,

Pope's couplet projects its formal symmetries on to the world of things and ideas that it mediates.

Davie's analysis is textualist in that he pays small attention to how and why external factors might have caused this change. Laura Brown (1985: 7) offers a contextualist explanation: 'Pope's art is at once a mode of representation and an act of adjudication through which an elaborate and sophisticated linguistic structure, emulative of the imperial age of Roman culture, shapes a "world" where rhetoric, belief and morality perfectly intersect'. Brown's main point is that Augustan poetry is influenced by the pervasive ideology of other contemporary discourses, all of which attempt to impose an idealized stability on the world. At one point (pp. 10–11) she compares a famous alliterative line from Pope's *The Rape of the Lock* (1712), 'Puffs, Powders, Patches, Bibles, Billet-doux' (I, 138), with a similar habit in the discourses of economic-political commentators to impose a subtle order of sound patterns on their lists of the commodities that were being brought to England during the new age of mercantile and colonial expansion. In a similar vein, Christopher Caudwell, a Marxist critic, proposed that the eighteenth-century 'closed' couplet reflected a contemporary obsession with import controls (1946: 46–8).

It could similarly be argued that the ungrounded diversity of functional and formal registers in Renaissance poetry is informed by the ideology of a state in a condition of change and uncertainty. The reigns of James I and Charles I, in which metaphysical poetry flourished, were years of tension between a network of economic, political and religious interests that would eventually lead to the Civil War.

The best-known textualist counterpart to this thesis is T. S. Eliot's concept of 'dissociation of sensibility' described in his essay on 'The Metaphysical Poets' (1921). Eliot argued that the metaphysicals, and Donne in particular, evolved a method of writing in which fields of perception and experience that rational thought encourages us to separate (reading, falling in love, eating) are in their poems, 'always forming new wholes', while the poets of the late seventeenth, eighteenth and nineteenth centuries caused their verse to reflect the dissociations and mechanical categorizations of rational discourse. Crucially Eliot identifies the cause of this change as a pattern of influences within the community and discourse of poetic writing (initiated by Dryden and Milton). In Eliot's model the changes that occurred in poetic style were influenced by the decisions of poets, not by the position of poetry within a broader impersonal discourse of ideological formations and hierarchies.

Linguistics offers us a model of historical change which provides another perspective on the contextualist–textualist divisions of literary stylistics. Saussure characterized language as both synchronic, a communication system at a particular point in history, and diachronic, a series of alterations and transformations of this system through history.

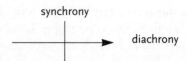

Jakobson and his colleague Mukarovsky regarded this clinical distinction between synchrony and diachrony as a methodological fiction. They argued that at any putative point in time on the diachronic scale there is a continuous tension between elements of the linguistic past and the present. Current shifts in linguistic usage (for example changes in pronunciation, the introduction of new semantic elements, idiomatic fashions) must be perceived in relation to elements of the linguistic past which remain unchanged. They restructured the diagram as shown on page 115.

What they sought to represent was language as a system which never immediately abandons its historical past. The changes along the diachronic scale from a to b to c are not absolute and final; instead they function as a thickening, an increase in the

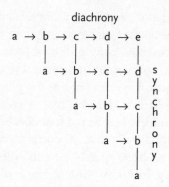

(see 'Der Struktur des Phonems', in Jakobson, 1971: 280–310)

complexity of an ever-changing synchronic continuum. A current example of this is the use of the word 'gay'. Its use as a familiar, idiomatic substitute for homosexual has effectively marginalized its previous semantic designation as happy or carefree. But the earlier usage has not been entirely displaced. It is sometimes used in its older context by people who object to its appropriation as a synonym, and its use in pre-1970s texts is often quoted as a joke – the questionable humour originating from the clash between diachronic and synchronic registers.

This way of perceiving the relation between synchrony and diachrony can be adapted to the more complex relation between history, text and context in literary studies. Saussure's model and its later adaptation to the so-called 'Prague Prism' (Jakobson and Mukarovsky were working in Prague at the time) is based upon the study of language *per se*. The contextual factors that influence or promote linguistic change affect the diagram but they are not part of it. In terms of literary history and stylistics, it would be more useful to regard the diachronic axis as consisting exclusively of the stylistic and structural features of literary texts, and the synchronic axis as involving an interface between non-literary discourses and systems of representation, and literary conventions and practices. At any point in time on the synchronic axis there is an interplay of the current or precedented conventions of literary style and the broader contextual continuum inhabited by the author and the reader. The diachronic axis concerns the progress and expansion of what literary style is and what literary style can do.

In the poems considered so far the functional register is related primarily to the synchronic axis. A poem such as 'The Relic' which attempts to replicate speech patterns will inevitably draw upon contemporary habits of elision, phraseology or diction. Demotic phrases such as 'make a little stay' or 'If this fall in a time, or land' would, by the end of the eighteenth century, have become conspicuously archaic. 'Stay' gradually lost its role as a combination of noun and intransitive verb (Donne's usage) and came to function only as one or the other (respectively 'your stay has been short' and 'can you stay?'); 'fall' is used by Donne as a substitute for the general verbal functions of 'occur', 'happen' or 'take place', but has, since the seventeenth century, become marginalized as a particular and limited temporal predicate ('my birthday falls in April'). In the early seventeenth century the term 'mis-devotion' (meaning Catholicism) would have evoked immediate and contemporary images of political conflict and potential war. The speaker's deployment of it in relation to his memories of the woman would, for a contemporary reader, further substantiate the impression of him as a real, troubled individual, given to using provocative and disturbing images.

The metrical framework for these functional registers belongs on the diachronic axis, and Jakobson has evolved a general formula for the relation between history and poetic form – the dominant.

> In the evolution of poetic form it is not so much a question of the disappearance of certain elements and the emergence of others as it is a question of shifts in the mutual relationships among the diverse

components of the system, in other words a question of the shifting dominant.

('The Dominant', in Jakobson, 1987: 44)

What Jakobson means is that whereas phrases such as 'make a little stay' will 'disappear' from the currency of ordinary speech, elements such as the relation between the heroic couplet and syntax in Donne and Pope are a function of a system of stylistic devices that will endure and expand.

The major landmarks in the progress of English poetry since the sixteenth century – the Renaissance, Augustan poetry, Romanticism, modernism – involve a variety of interfaces with their respective contexts. Pope's 'The Dunciad', Blake's 'London' and Eliot's *The Waste Land* present images of urban life, political and cultural questions and linguistic usages that are unique to the broader context of each poem. However, each poem draws upon what is essentially the same evolving system of intrinsically poetic devices. The system will acquire new elements – the non-dramatic usage of blank verse was effectively instituted by Milton's *Paradise Lost* and free verse was an invention of modernism – but this process of accumulation will not be matched by disappearances. Additions to the system might be prompted by the conditions of a specific moment in literary history, but thereafter they can be drawn upon and combined with other elements irrespective of what a particular poet wants to say about his/her personal experiences or historical circumstances. For example the poems of W. H. Auden are firmly situated in the poet's own experience of language, politics, social convention, sexuality and philosophy in post-1930s Europe and America. Auden draws upon practically the entire repertoire of stanzaic and metrical formulae, including free verse, that constitutes the system of English poetic form from the Renaissance to the mid-twentieth century. Jakobson does not propose that the intrinsically poetic system employed by a text will inevitably 'dominate' or obscure that text's relation to its period; the system is 'dominant' only in the sense that it is capable of preserving itself against the disappearances that feature in the history of non-poetic language.

Jakobson is a textualist. A contextualist model of literary style and history emerges from Roger Fowler's *Literature as Social Discourse*:

> [Literature] is an open set of texts, of great formal diversity, recognised by a culture as possessing certain institutional values and performing certain functions . . . the values are neither universal, though they are subject to a small range of types of historical explanation, nor stable, although they change slowly.
>
> (1981: 81)

Fowler shifts the perspective on literature away from Jakobson's concept of the diachronic axis as a 'system', and towards the social and cultural values that affect literature at any given historical point. He does not deny that literature has certain intrinsic features, but he regards the effects created by these as contingent upon the historically variable perceptions of what literature is and what literature does:

> They [the perceived values of literature] derive from the economic and social structures of particular societies . . . . My aim here is not to promulgate Marxist explanations, but to suggest that once we start looking at literature as part of social process then texts are opened to the same kinds of causal and functional interpretations as are found in the sociology of language generally.
>
> (ibid.)

Jakobson and Fowler agree that literature is stylistically different from other linguistic discourses, but Fowler sees those differences as a function of historically determined acts of intention and interpretation while Jakobson is more concerned with the distinct evolutionary progress of literature *per se*. In the rest of this Part I shall consider both perspectives.

8

SHAKESPEARE'S DRAMA: TWO STYLISTIC REGISTERS

Practically all of Shakespeare's plays are comprised of two very different stylistic patterns: verse and unversified speech. We can make a number of reasonably straightforward observations about the reason for using blank verse and prosaic speech in the same text. Often the distinction between blank verse and prose mirrors the distinction between the social status and behavioural patterns of the characters. Those characters who hold an executive role both in the narrative and as representatives of their counterparts in the real world tend to communicate with one another more in blank verse than in prose. We might thus conclude that Shakespeare maintains the status of poetry as part of a complex series of sign systems – including dress, demeanour, names, occupations – that allow us to recognize strata within a particular social hierarchy. Poetry is culture: it is a linguistic form which disposes a collective identity on its users – and we should here recall that the speaker of 'The Relic' foregrounds his self-conscious sophistication in the claim that he has by this 'paper [poem] taught'. In sharing a certain code they can be seen as sharing a particular set of privileges, responsibilities, intellectual and moral concerns. Spoken, prose discourse does not even demand literacy. It is a means of exchange, dependent upon circumstances, and in the plays it occurs frequently in the exchanges between the low-life characters of the sub-plot.

The following is from Act I, scene ii of *Measure for Measure* (1604) in which Claudio, the young gentleman, tells Lucio, the resourceful opportunist, of his arrest for having had pre-marital sex with his fiancée.

LUCIO   Why, how now, Claudio! Whence comes this restraint?

CLAUDIO   From too much liberty, my Lucio, liberty:
         As surfeit is the father of much fast
         So every scope by the immoderate use
         Turns to restraint. Our natures do pursue –
         Like rats that ravin down their proper bane –
         A thirsty evil, and when we drink we die.

LUCIO   If I could speak so wisely under an arrest, I would send
         for certain of my creditors. And yet, to say the truth, I had
         as lief have the foppery of freedom as the morality of
         imprisonment. What's thy offence, Claudio?

Claudio's answer to Lucio's first enquiry is a masterpiece of poetic self-reference. The question, 'Whence comes this restraint?' is prompted by the actual and observable circumstances of Claudio being in the custody of the Provost and his officers. Instead of answering directly, Claudio uses the question as the basis for an elaborate pattern of rhetorical figures, a combination of euphuism (the extended use of balance and paradox), synoeciosis (an expanded paradox), *progressio* (advancing by steps of a comparison), and syncrisis (comparing contrary elements in contrasting clauses): all interlaced with metaphor. Restraint is the consequence of too much liberty: surfeit is the father of fast; immoderate scope causes restraint. Natural (unrestrained) thirst is, like rats who eat their young, a dangerous evil: when we drink we die.

This impressive display of figures is enclosed within the metrical and syntactic conventions of blank verse, and the passage should remind us of Donne's and Herbert's poems: why is a functional, emotive expression bound into a self-consciously complex, unspontaneous structure? This question is taken up by Lucio, who is as puzzled by Claudio's use of poetic language as he is by his physical circumstances. 'Speak so wisely' is an ironic reference to the cultural status of poetry: it is a discourse in which the actualities of life are submitted to the reflective mood of wisdom, not a form of expression Lucio would expect from a man 'under an arrest'.

Throughout the scene there is a palpable tension between Lucio's attempts to ground the exchange in the specifics of the situation (why are you under arrest? what will you do about it?) and Claudio's extrapolation of these details into poetic reflections upon existence, identity, fate and justice.

Measure for Measure is an important play because it deliberately foregrounds the relationship between literary style and the broader functional purposes of language in society, politics and the law. It was first performed in 1604 for the new monarch, James I. James was the author of a political tract called *Basilikon Doron* (1599) in which he argued that a monarch should tread cautiously between his status as the executive embodiment of law and governance and his function as a moderator, an arbiter between the often divergent interests and perceptions of his people. The Duke in *Measure for Measure* plays out this double role. For most of the play he operates in disguise as a mysterious friar, suggesting strategies and deceptions through which the imbalance between the letter of the law and its just and practical implementation might be resolved. Along with his skills in physical role-play he is able to move comfortably between the two stylistic and cultural registers of blank verse and prose. In Act III, scene i the Duke 'as a friar' comforts Claudio in his death cell. Their exchange is followed by one between Claudio and his sister Isabella, a novitiate nun who has been offered the chance to save her brother's life by submitting to the sexual advances of Angelo, the temporary head of state. She explains to Claudio that her refusal to do so is a matter of sacred principle: her virginity and her vows are more valuable than her, and his, life. The two exchanges between Claudio and the Duke and Claudio and Isabella are conducted in blank verse. Like all dialogic exchanges the substance of each statement is determined partly by what has been said by the other speaker and partly by the two speakers' perceptions of the issues and context of the exchange. At the same time, each speaker is embedded in a discourse with specific rules and preconditions; if one speaker ends in the middle of a pentameter the other will complete it. The stylistic particulars of poetry do not in themselves impose an excessive restriction on what can and cannot be said, but its status as a discourse in which the referent or subject becomes the basis for elaborate figurative speculation seems to encourage the speakers to create their own self-referring lyrics: in Jakobson's terms the speaker is 'split' between the pragmatics of the one-to-one exchange and the opportunity for a complex reflection on their circumstances. For example in the middle of their exchange on the balance between honourable behaviour and opportunism Claudio launches into a lengthy discourse on the meaning of death:

> Ay, but to die, and go we know not where;
> To lie in cold obstruction and to rot;
> This sensible warm motion to become
> A kneaded clod; and the delighted spirit
> To bathe in fiery floods, or to reside
> In thrilling region of thick-ribbed ice . . .
>
> (Act III, scene i, lines 116–21)

Such extra-dialogic excursions are a common feature of Renaissance drama, but they are significantly absent from the second part of the scene, in prose, where the Duke proposes to Isabella a means of effectively blackmailing Angelo into commuting Claudio's sentence. In this part the substance of the information exchanged is the governing stylistic feature.

> DUKE . . . Have you not heard speak of Mariana, the sister of
> Frederick, the great soldier who miscarried at sea?
> ISABELLA I have heard of the lady, and good words went with her
> name.
> DUKE She should this Angelo have married; was affianced to her by
> oath, and the nuptial appointed.
>
> (lines 215–22)

Throughout the dialogue speculations on morality, existence, justice, life and death are marginalized by the swift and effective transference of details and ideas: Angelo has reneged on his engagement; Isabella and the abandoned Mariana can trap him with the famous 'bed trick'.

It would be possible to rewrite the two parts of the scene: to reduce the Claudio–Isabella exchange to a yes–no prose argument about the practicalities and benefits of submitting to Angelo and to allow the Duke and Isabella to speculate in verse on the broader moral and philosophical resonances of Angelo and the bed trick. Shakespeare's choice of stylistic-contextual matching is prompted by the practicalities of characterization and plot. Isabella will never compromise her own moral and spiritual condition – hence the dialogue is non-functional, speculative, poetic – while Angelo can be influenced by his amoral, opportunistic activities – the dialogue is governed by the specifics of detail and event.

Erich Auerbach in *Mimemis* (1946) has shown that while Shakespeare draws upon the localized devices of rhetoric and the broader conventions of classical drama and epic narrative, he also mixes them, allowing aristocratic 'heroic' characters to share the idioms and sometimes the habits and problems of the lower orders. Auerbach suggests that this genre-mixing is mimetic in the sense that the social and hierarchical structures of late sixteenth-century England had become much more fluid and less predictable than those of the feudal period. He emphasizes character and situation as mimetic keystones, but, by contrast, Mikhail Bakhtin (1934–5) looks more closely at the ideological resonances of literary and non-literary style. Poetry, Bakhtin argues, is a 'unifying and centralising . . . force of verbal and ideological life'. He does not suggest that poetry is or can be an instrument of social or ideological enforcement; rather that its sense of formal cohesion, its stylistic difference from the context-influenced style of non-poetic language, indicates a model of thought and behaviour that is uncontaminated by the dangerous contingencies of ordinary life. Prose, on the other hand, has 'historically taken form in the current of decentralizing, centrifugal forces' (ibid.: 86).

The Duke embodies a political message, roughly corresponding to King James's *Basilikon Doron*: he shows that the contingent opportunism of the lower orders (such as the bed trick) cannot be separated entirely from the abstract philosophizing of the ruling classes. But just as significantly, his nimble shifts between blank verse and prose demonstrate that literary mimesis operates as an axis between the linguistic registers of the real world (prose) and the stylistic conventions that are specific to literature (blank verse).

Practically all literary texts of the Renaissance defer to the hierarchical relation between poetic and non-poetic language: the double pattern operates as a compositional framework. Indeed, the play with which Shakespeare may have concluded his career as a dramatist, *The Tempest* (1611), is a self-conscious acknowl-edgement of this dynamic relationship. It begins with prose. The dialogic exchanges between Alonso, Gonzalo, Antonio, and the seamen are governed by a single, pervasive referent, the storm.

This first act replicates the conditions and effects of the dialogue between the Duke and Isabella: style is determined by immediate circumstantial events. The poetic function of the play is controlled by Prospero. He rules the island, and orchestrates the apparently contingent events that affect the activities of its inhabitants. The obvious allegorical parallel is between Prospero and the playwright, but the play's allegorical resonance has been traced beyond this to contemporary accounts of voyages to what were to become the first English colonies in the Caribbean and North America. Stephen Greenblatt (1990: 24) has argued that the allegorical puzzles raised by the play disclose the new phenomenon of colonialism as 'a problematical model for the theatrical imagination'. For stylistics the most significant feature of the play is its use of the blank verse/prose division as a device for framing and foregrounding its broader, allegorical resonances. For example, Caliban is the archetype of ignoble savagery, a figure with human sensibilities, but with roots at the lower, bestial end of the scale of being. Caliban detests his master, Prospero, and is convinced that Prospero's power lies in his learning: 'his books; for without them/He's but as sot, as I am' (Act III, scene ii, lines 103–4). Paradoxically, Caliban speaks only in blank verse, that stylistic symbol of high culture and sophistication. He does not choose to do so, but Prospero has taught him only this form of language, and there is a bizarre sequence (Act III, scene ii) in which Caliban converses in blank verse with Trinculo (jester) and Stephano (drunken butler) whose social positions are firmly situated in prose.

> TRINCULO I did not give thee the lie: – Out o' your wits and hearing
> too? – A pox o' your bottle! This can sack and drinking do – A
> murrain on your monster, and the devil take your fingers!
> CALIBAN Ha, ha ha!
> STEPHANO Now forward with your tale – Prithee stand further off.
> CALIBAN Beat him enough: after a little time
>   I'll beat him too

STEPHANO   Stand further – Come, proceed.

CALIBAN   Why, as I told thee, 'tis a custom with him
                  I' the afternoon to sleep: there thou may'st brain him,
                  Having first seiz'd his books; or with a log
                  Batter his skull

(Act III, scene ii, lines 88–101)

What Caliban has to suggest regarding the planned assault upon Prospero is not elevated by moral, ethical or even emotional reflections, and in this respect his message is well suited to the disorderly, opportunistic context he shares with his new companions. At the same time, however, his speech carries stylistic signals that are at odds with his setting and his message. The enjambed phrase 'or with a log/Batter his skull' reflects a mind conditioned to the habits of shaping language to the high-cultural conventions of blank verse. Caliban's emotional universe may stretch no further than the desire to cause pain, but while expressing this desire he takes care to place the noun-instrument 'log' at the final stress position of the line and to open the next line with a trochaic stress reversal, 'Báttēr', which emphasizes the purposive anger of the main verb. Prospero, his victim, has instructed him well in the stylistics of high culture.

It might be argued that Shakespeare is making a statement about the arbitrary nature of language and its generic divisions: anyone can be taught blank verse but such an acquired competence does not guarantee the qualities of nobility, wisdom or sophistication with which poetry was associated – in contemporary rhetorical terms Caliban has *oratio* (speech) without *ratio* (reason). In a broader sense, however, we should recognize that Shakespeare is, as in *Measure for Measure*, making use of exclusively literary devices as a means of engaging with issues and events that lie outside the text; principally the new age of seaborne exploration, early colonization and the distinction between European civilization and the savages of the new world.

One of the few plays of the period to consist entirely of unpoetic dialogue is Ben Jonson's *Bartholomew Fair* (1614). In this the hierarchy of poetic and non-poetic discourses that conventionally provides the axis between text and context has been abandoned. The stylistic foreground is occupied instead by dialect, slang, the idiolect and catchwords of the everyday exchanges of the ordinary people of London.

The novel, born in the eighteenth century, would eventually incorporate elements of both texts. The narrator of the novel would, like Prospero, migrate between the roles of participant in, orchestrator and creator of the narrative. And, like Jonson, the novelist would draw upon the unrefined substance of ordinary speech and dialogue. It would be foolish to argue that the novel was the offspring of interbred Renaissance conventions (although, as we shall see, Fielding the novelist learnt a lot from Fielding the comic dramatist). But it would be equally foolish to ignore these intertextual relations and transformations and regard the novel solely as the product of contextual determinants.

9

THE EIGHTEENTH- AND NINETEENTH-CENTURY NOVEL

The term 'intertextuality' was introduced first into French criticism in the late 1960s by Julia Kristeva (1969) in her discussion and elaboration of Bakhtin's principle of dialogism (see above, pp. 83–4). Kristeva argued that no text is 'free' of other texts; that the generic difference between communicative types – novels, letters, essays, poems, plays – is overridden by their dialogic, intertextual relationship. Intertextuality offers a useful model for an understanding of how the novel transformed and unsettled the relatively stable balance between the literary (poetic) and non-literary registers of Renaissance texts. As we saw in Part I, the novel is an all-inclusive framework of genres and linguistic styles. Anything made of language can appear in a novel. The narrator might offer us a facsimile of a signpost, a menu, a letter or a newspaper article; human thoughts, opinions and activities are mediated through dialogue, internal and external focalization and interior monologue.

The English novel was born in the eighteenth century but its parentage is uncertain. Unlike Renaissance poetry it could not draw upon an established stylistic and rhetorical tradition. There were many texts, literary and non-literary, which included narrative, but their stylistic affiliations were various and marginal. Epic or narrative poems such as those of Homer and Virgil, or more recently those of Spenser and Milton, balanced their storyline against inclusive and persistent poetic structures. The Bible and scripture used prose narrative but, like histories and chronicles, stylistic and structural presentation was predicated upon theological or chronological truths. Writers such as George Gascoigne (*A Hundreth Sundrie Flowres*, 1573), Thomas Nashe (*The Unfortunate Traveller*, 1594) and Thomas Deloney (*Jack of Newberie*, 1597) had published fictional prose tales, but prior to the early eighteenth century there was no established tradition of extended narrative in prose which drew upon contemporary events, habits and conditions and made no claims to extra-linguistic authenticity or truth. As a consequence, fiction began to make use of a complicated mixture of stylistic registers, drawing selectively upon literary and non-literary discourses.

In what follows I shall consider examples of this type of predatory stylistics and also look at how the novel began to evolve its own typology of stylistic conventions. In short, intertextuality operates for prose fiction in two ways: the novel is a pluralistic discourse in which otherwise distinct genres and communicative functions exist in the same text, but at the same time the novel eventually established an intertextual tradition in which novels fed upon and altered the characteristics of their predecessors.

Before considering the novel as a separate genre I will deal with a text that both reflects and problematizes the notion of inter-textuality. Swift's *A Modest Proposal* (1729) was published seven years after Daniel Defoe's *Moll Flanders*, but it is not regarded as a novel. Its stylistic character places it firmly in the generic sphere of the political tract and the journalistic essay. It does not tell a story. It addresses itself to a particular socio-economic theme – poverty in Ireland – and it proposes a solution – the sale of the children of the poor as meat. *A Modest Proposal* is reprinted and taught as a literary text, as a prose counterpart to the satirical tradition of the public poem. How is it that a text which appears to involve none of the defining stylistic features of literature (including the novel) is perceived as a literary work?

In order to address this question we should first investigate its premise: is there any stylistic evidence that *A Modest Proposal* is literature? In order to do this we need to turn back to Jakobson's diagram of the communicative circuit (p. 41). The context of Swift's text is announced in its title:

A Modest Proposal for preventing the Children of poor People in Ireland, from being a Burden to their Parents or Country; and for making them beneficial to the Publick.

The title assumes an awareness on the part of the reader of the socio-economic situation in Ireland, and signals the type of discourse in which the writer considers problems and projects solutions. This mode of political tract was common in the early eighteenth century and its code and contact function were well established. Its code is its style, the most consistent feature of which is the predication of a subject or referent of which it is assumed that the reader will have some basic knowledge and upon which the referential features of each sentence (mainly the noun phrases) will depend. In the opening three paragraphs Swift's projector offers a detailed consideration of poverty in Dublin, with specific reference to 'this prodigious number of Children in arms' as the main cause of urban destitution. His persistent use of the definite article ('this great Town', 'these Children', 'these Mothers') assumes a shared awareness of the subject. The contact function is the related assumption that the reader will be familiar with the subjects and conventions of the political tract. When the projector states that 'I have always found [other projectors] grossly mistaken in their computation' he is confident that the reader will have engaged in similar discourses.

Jakobson's point was that if the message of a text were bound into the poetic function then contact, code and context would be drawn away from their functional, real-world operations and into the literary framework of the text: we have seen a similar integration of text and context occur in prose fiction. In *A Modest Proposal* there seem to be no obvious stylistic signals of literary writing, but let us recall Genette's notion of focalization as the stylistic common denominator of fiction. Focalization refers to the 'angle of vision' which permeates the fabric of a novel. It situates the narrator as a presence who occupies a middle ground between the known opinions and circumstances of the real author and the created world of the text, and there is evidence that Swift's projector functions in this way.

The first eight paragraphs of the tract are concerned with establishing the conditions of poverty in Ireland: the solution is alluded to indirectly as 'a fair, cheap and easy method', 'my Intention', 'my Thoughts', 'my Scheme'. The projector makes an intriguing reference to boys and girls as a 'saleable commodity', but this could be the figurative language of hard economics – labour is capital. It is only after 1,000 words that we encounter the phrases 'young healthy child' and 'wholesome food'. This is the paragraph in which the 'proposal' is specified.

> I have been assured by a very knowing American of my acquaintance in London, that a young healthy Child well Nursed is at a year old a most delicious nourishing and wholesome Food, whether Stewed, Roasted, Baked, or Boiled; and I make no doubt that it will equally serve in a Fricassee or Ragout.

The deep structure, the main clause, of this sentence is: 'I have been assured that a one year old child is [good] food'. The relative clauses are numerous and effectively swamp the main clause: the source of the assurance (the American); the health and nursing of the child; the quality of the food; the manner of cooking; and the presentation of the dish. This syntactic embedding of the main clause in a variety of relative clauses is the basis of a broader thematic and structural pattern which permeates the entire text. The actuality of the proposal, eating people, resonates through the text as a kind of ghostly main clause. Direct verbal and nominal references to eating children are rare. Instead the text bombards the reader with disquisitions on familiar topics that have no precedented connection with cannibalism: agriculture, finance, Catholicism, the commercial expansion of England, culinary niceties, the human condition. The bizarre and disturbing image of the sale, butchering and preparation of children is cautiously and briefly introduced and exists for most of the text in the mind of the reader, who is obliged to integrate it with the more comfortable and conventional subjects of the political tract or the journalistic essay.

If we subject Swift's projector to the same functionalist model that we employed with Donne's addresser in 'The Relic' we find a similar tension between text and context. On the one hand the projector is presented as an informed commentator on economics and politics who assumes a comparable level of learning and interest on the part of his readers. But this level of interactive discourse between projector and reader is unsettled by the indirect, circular manner in which the projector specifies his 'scheme'. Selling and eating children is a new feature of contemporary political discourse yet the projector treats it as a natural and logical condition of the ethos he shares with the reader. Most readers, we assume, would be rather shocked by the projector's scheme, but no assumed expectation of the reader's surprise nor any provision of a moral or ethical framework to appease the reader's possible sense of unease will be found in the text.

In 'The Relic' our perception of the speaker and the utterance as real and improvised is unsettled by the stylistic artifice of the text. In *A Modest Proposal* the imbalance between text and context is caused by the use of a familiar channel of discourse whose stylistic and referential framework remain undisturbed by the shocking and unprecedented nature of the message. From the point of view of stylistics the text is significant because it employs a literary device – an unsettling juxtaposition of genre, message and context – by drawing upon a contemporary discourse whose primary function involves the circulation of non-literary ideas and propositions. The contemporary novelist was similarly involved in the meshing of literary and non-literary discourses, styles and structural frameworks.

The narrator of Fielding's *Tom Jones* (1749) never discloses any actual or biographical involvement with the characters or events of the story, but he addresses the reader as though he/she were someone sitting opposite in the office, house or drawing room. Fielding's narrator will often begin a chapter with sentences such as 'My reader may please to remember he hath been informed that Jenny Jones . . . ' (Book 2, Chapter 3) or 'For the reasons mentioned in the preceding chapter, and from some other matrimonial concessions . . . ' (Book 2, Chapter 4). This method recalls the conversational manner of Addison's *Spectator* essays: 'Having in my yesterday's paper considered . . . ' (no. 171, Saturday 15 September). The regular, daily appearance of Addison's articles enabled him to set aside the printed impersonality of the form and engage the reader in the one-to-one deictics of 'yesterday's paper'. Fielding's narrator achieves a similar though far more complex conflation of the spatio-temporal deictics of the narrative with a sense of the characters and events narrated as part of a real continuum of experience which he shares with the reader – a peculiar meshing of Shklovsky's notions of *fabula* and *sjuzet*.

He begins Book 15, Chapter 10 with, 'The letter, then, which arrived at the end of the preceding chapter was from Mr Allworthy . . . '. Substitute 'yesterday morning' for 'the preceding chapter' and he could be referring to an actual event occurring at a place and time familiar to addresser and addressee. The uneasy relation between location and time as real elements and as structural features of the text is a pervasive element of Fielding's novel. He begins Book 10, Chapter 8 by advising the reader to 'look a little back' to be 'pleased to remember that, in the ninth chapter of the seventh book of our history, we left Sophia, after a long debate between love and duty, deciding the cause . . . '. Unlike an actual addressee, the reader does not need to 'remember'; we can turn the pages. This uncertain relation between reality and fiction is maintained through the narrator's account of the encounters between Blifil, the squire and Mrs Western. He begins by recollecting the events as a single, completed sequence ('This debate *had* arisen'; 'there *was not* a single person sober'; '*it had* the evening before *been* fixed'), gradually adjusts the tense so that the events are brought closer to the present ('Breakfast was now set forth in the parlour') and eventually achieves a balance between the present and the immediate past ('"Not to be found!" cries the squire, starting from his chair'; '"La! brother," said Mrs Western'). Throughout the chapter the narrator maintains an uneasy position between omniscience (he seems to know what the characters are thinking) and the position of someone who can only relate the events in relation to their own largely unpredictable order. For example, the squire 'sat himself contentedly down' in the parlour and nothing much happens between this and the point at which 'the report was brought from the garden . . . that Madame Sophia was not to be found'. The time between the two events appears to allow the narrator the opportunity to digress on the inclinations and talents of the characters involved. The narrator seems on the one hand to command a superhuman perspective upon his narrative: he describes the physical appearance and exact location and movement around the house of all the characters in a way that would in the real world involve him being in several places at the same time. On the other hand, he seems to find it necessary to tailor his account of the dialogue and events to their actual temporal progress.

In the 1740s there was no well-established narrative tradition upon which Fielding could base his method of integrating the deictics of fiction with the immediacy of non-fictional discourse, and it could be argued that his narrator's curious position of being at once within and outside the narrative was an inter-textual borrowing from Fielding's earlier career as a dramatist. The temporal sequence of the actors'/characters' movements determines the dialogue and the progression of the plot, but the third-person narrative enables Fielding to offer the reader a perspective on the events and characters that is denied to the dramatist and his audience.

The problem that faced the eighteenth-century novelist was of how exactly the multi-generic elements and spatio-temporal conditions of the novel should be sewn together as a narrative structure. The epistolary novel was a frequently used mode: letters are in themselves multi-generic discourses, capable of including reflective speculations, pleas, stories, orders, reported speech and characterization. However, in these the novelist had to combine the mimetic one-to-one discourse of the individual letter with a thread of narrative continuity that would carry the reader from letter to letter. Often the seams of the narrative fabric would begin to show. The following is from Samuel Richardson's epistolary novel *Pamela* (1740–1):

> So so! Where will this end? – Mrs Jewkes has been with me from him, and she says, I must get out of the house this moment . . . there is, I see, the chariot drawn out, the horses too, the grim Colbrand going to get on horseback. What will be the end of all this?

Like his contemporary, Fielding, Richardson is stretched between the various levels and demands of fictional mimesis. It is implausible to imagine that someone could orchestrate the writing of a letter with a second-by-second account of events taking place outside the window, but Richardson clearly felt the need to foreground activities that lay behind the exchange of the letters.

Laurence Sterne's *Tristram Shandy* (1759–67) is a first-person narrative, and Sterne's use of this technique discloses what was at that time its unrefined flexibility. Shandy's narrative can best be described as parenthetic. He tells stories, but he never allows the reader to properly disentangle the objective nature of the tale from the memories, interruptions, digressions and immediate concerns of the teller.

> Every day for at least ten years together did my father resolve to have it mended, – 'tis not mended yet; – no family but ours would have borne with it an hour, – and what is most astonishing, there was not a subject in the world upon which my father was so eloquent, as upon that of door-hinges.
>
> (Vol. III, Chapter 21)

The ostensible subject of this mini-narrative is the faulty parlour door, but the stylistic pattern is so embedded in digressions on the habits of Shandy's father, their origins and philosophic promptings, that the actual subject is the immediate thoughts and opinions of Tristram Shandy. By the end of the novel the reader is left with an untidy combination of anecdotes, reflections, enquiries and propositions, but nothing that resembles a single purposive plot. And again we find that the non-literary registers of linguistic interaction – in this case the experience of listening to Shandy's unplanned digressive discourse – are as significant a stylistic feature as any established typology of narrative conventions.

Shklovsky celebrated Sterne's exposure of the uncertain relation between storytelling (*sjuzet*) and the story (*fabula*), but we should recognize that Sterne's perverse and individual style was not too far removed from the more conventional, though equally exploratory, techniques of Fielding and Richardson. All draw upon a broad network of genres and discourses, but in the eighteenth century the rules governing their combination in fictional texts were flexible and uncertain.

There was no specific moment at which the English novel

acquired a cohesive grammar or typology of stylistic conventions, but Victorian fiction is certainly more confidently aware of its own stylistic character than was its eighteenth-century predecessor. Compare our discussion of Fielding with our earlier analysis of some of the features of Jane Austen's *Northanger Abbey* (pp. 61–3). In Austen's novel the relationship between the focalizing agent, the narrator, and the focalizer, Catherine, creates a narrative structure which draws upon, selects and organizes the temporal and spatial conditions of the narrated events. The narrator cautiously orchestrates accounts of Catherine's feelings with a selective fabric of past events, immediate occurrences and likely prospects. Fielding's narrator is constantly adjusting and reframing the narrative, often with apologies to the reader, in accordance with events that seem to be operating beyond his controlling presence.

In Defoe's *Moll Flanders* (1722) Moll's first-person account is predominantly in the past tense, but she never allows the benefits of retrospective distance to obscure the immediacy of her report. Whether, as in the final pages, she is describing her husband's reaction to the practicalities of the voyage back to England or, at the beginning of her story, telling of her mother's conviction for petty theft, the reader gets the impression that the events have only just occurred. Often, when reporting dialogue, Moll will shift unpredictably between the past and present tense:

> 'Why', says I, 'tis a little hand upon me . . .'
> 'Well', says he, 'Captain – may have told me so . . . '
> 'That is so just', said I, 'and so generous . . . '
> 'The less you have, my dear', says he . . .
>
> (Penguin edn, 1978: 79)

This could be viewed as a naturalistic strategy – Moll is attempting to keep her account alive, to involve the reader in its immediacy – and it indicates that Defoe is employing stylistic devices in order to reconcile the structure of a fictional text with the communicative conventions of non-fictional discourse. His task is difficult, because the reader of *Moll Flanders* is left in an uneasy position between immediacy and recollection and is faced with attendant questions. How can she remember these events and conversations so well? She cannot, through her career as prostitute, convict and deportee, have kept a diary. How is it, we wonder, that she has such a precise memory of the £93 cost of a twelve-day 'ramble' through Oxford (ibid.: 9), of how her husband 'pawned twenty pieces of fine holland for £30 which were really worth above £90' (ibid.: 80), of how each move to a lodging house or new address by her herself or her acquaintances took place in exact relation to this or that event on the preceding or following day?

Dickens, in writing *Great Expectations* (1861), faced the same problem of reconciling thirty years of events, experiences and their emotional effects with the notion of their recollection and reconstruction as a single retrospective narrative. At the beginning of his story, Pip tells of his first meeting with Magwitch and of his theft of the pork pie:

> The mist was heavier yet when I got out upon the marshes, so that instead of my running at everything, everything seemed to run at me. This was very disagreeable to a guilty mind. The gates and dykes and banks came bursting at me through the mist, as if they cried as plainly as could be, 'A body with Somebody-else's pork pie! Stop him!' The cattle came upon me with like suddenness, staring out of their eyes, and steaming out of their nostrils, 'Halloa, young thief!' One black ox, with a white cravat on – who even had to my awakened conscience something of a clerical air – fixed me so obstinately with his eyes, and moved his blunt head around in such an accusatory manner as I moved round, that I blubbered out to him, 'I couldn't help it, sir! It wasn't for myself I took it!'
>
> (Chapter 3)

Dickens creates a subtle merger between the adult Pip, narrator and focalizer, and Pip the child, subject of the narrative and focalizing agent. The passage sustains a single figurative device: the younger Pip's surroundings are variously mobilized and personified as agents of justice and retribution. This works well in situating the reader in the experience of the child. The gates, dykes, banks and cattle as pursuers and accusers is a mental image that one might expect from a combination of ingenuous tension and unsophisticated guilt. At the same time the experience and mind of the young focalizer are assimilated to the stylistic and ratiocinative complexities of the adult narrator. The black ox with the white 'cravat' might well have had a subliminal effect upon the nervous boy, but only the adult could construct the figurative and resonant phrase, 'who even had to my awakened conscience something of a clerical air'. Dickens has established a discourse between narrator and narratee in accordance with Chatman's diagram (p. 55). Here a shared familiarity is assumed with the image of the clergyman as the symbolic regulator of a society's moral code, and although the spatio-temporal deictics of the scene focus on the experience of the child, the system of discourse and focalization appropriates this experience as part of the conventions and expectations of an adult.

The novel describes the experiences of Pip from childhood to maturity and throughout the text we are aware that the older Pip – in Chatman's terms, the narrator and implied author – is constantly selecting and refining recollected events and emotions. He uses the narrative structure as a means of integrating memories with his current temperamental and emotional condition, and we should recognize that eighteenth-century novelists, such as Defoe, had not developed the complex and subtle relation between implied author and narrative that emerges in *Great Expectations*. This brings us to the relation between the stylistic character of a text and its ability to reflect and mediate the conditions of its age; in short, realism.

The polished, confident mode of Victorian fiction is often referred to as classic realism. The concept was first used by Barthes in *S/Z* (1970), popularized by Catherine Belsey (1980), and in general terms it refers to the acquisition by the nineteenth-century novel of a formal and stylistic character that is comparable with the rules and conventions that genres such as poetry inherited from their classical antecedents. It is argued that one of the effects of this is that the novel, like poetry, becomes a genre whose developed techniques of refraction and mediation effectively distance it from the disorders and tensions of non-literary discourses and experience. The eighteenth-century novel was an experimental form. Richardson, Fielding and Tobias Smollett engaged with the formulae of first and third person and epistolary narrative but there were very few precedents and no properly established conventions governing the deployment of these techniques. As we have seen, the relationship between the form of the novel and its use of non-literary discourse, such as reported speech, was, in the eighteenth century, flexible and sometimes unpredictable. The eighteenth-century novel could be regarded as realistic in that its unfixed conventions allowed it to respond in very different ways to linguistic registers that operated in everyday life. Victorian classic realism differed from this: nineteenth-century novelists operated within tacitly agreed conventions through which non-literary discourses and reported events would be processed by the structural features of the text. This was not simply a stylistic development. The Victorian novel stood at the borderline between popular culture and literary art. Both were closely monitored by and indeed complicit with the moral and ethical codes that permeated practically all levels, and certainly all published work, of Victorian society. Classic realism denotes, in one sense, the development of the novel into a stylistic form with agreed structures and conventions comparable with those of 'classical' literature, mostly poetry. More significantly, the classic realist novel, in its various stylistic and referential permutations, became a function of what could and what could not be said in print.

This case is stated succinctly by Leo Bersani (1978: 62–3):

> The formal and psychological reticence of most realistic fiction makes for a secret complicity between the novelist and his society's illusions about its own order. Realistic fiction serves nineteenth century society by providing it with strategies for containing (and repressing) its disorder within significantly structured stories about itself.

What Bersani means is that the stylistic congruences of novels such as *Great Expectations* enable the novelist to impose a formal and aesthetic order upon his/her source material, and the social and ideological conditions of Victorian England are certainly well served by these stylistic developments. Sexual desire and activity, for example, could only be reconciled with nineteenth-century public discourse by means of symbol, euphemism or scriptural invocation. Pip's cautious, selective integration of events and dialogue with narrative discourse offers Dickens what is effectively a form of censorship, whereas eighteenth-century novels, which involved a more flexible, less co-ordinated relation between narrative and external habits and discourses, often incorporated explicit descriptions and reported discussions of sexual activity. The bodily manifestations, effects and consequences of sexual desire are, in Victorian fiction, obliquely inferred or ambiguously symbolized.

Colin MacCabe (1978: 36) argues that the Victorian novelist, specifically George Eliot, is 'devoted to repressing the operations of the signifier by positing a metalanguage which exists outside of materiality and production. The multitude of objects that appear in her texts do not bear witness to the activity of signification.' 'Metalanguage' is effectively the narrative. In Jakobson's diagram (p. 41) the term refers to the ways in which different codes can be used to address the same topic. In MacCabe's model the metalinguistic code is the narrative structure of the novel which, he argues, is not merely a different method of mediating the dynamics of real life or 'the activity of signification', but in effect a means of distorting, censoring and 'repressing' them.

MacCabe's point is that Eliot, and other Victorian novelists, used the stylistic sophistication of the novel as an ideological tool. In the eighteenth century the metalanguage of the text, 'the text outside the area of inverted commas', had functioned as a flexible, responsive structure which engaged with codes, genres and discourses drawn from the world outside the text. In the nineteenth century, however, the metalanguage of the narrative organizes 'a specific hierarchy of discourses which places the reader in a position of dominance with regard to the stories and characters' (ibid.: 18). The reader, via the narrative, is offered a coherent model of reality which corresponds with a generally middle-class ideal of social, ethical and moral codes.

The narrators of *Middlemarch* (1871–2) and *Tom Jones* share a number of characteristics. Both engage the reader in a one-to-one discourse which presupposes shared interests and intellectual concerns, and both use this as an axis between the world inhabited by reader and narrator and the fictional world of the novel. However, the narrator of *Tom Jones* seems able only to disclose and comment on the moral condition or social ambition of the novel's characters, while George Eliot's narrator will frequently juxtapose an apparently objective report of a character's history, thoughts and words with elaborate disquisitions in which she shares with the reader the problem of reconciling unquestioned moral and philosophic absolutes with the complexities of her story. The opening sentence of Chapter 55 is typical: 'If youth is the season of hope, it is often so only in the sense that our elders are hopeful about us; for no age is so apt as youth to think its emotions, partings, and resolves are the last of their kind.' This discussion of age and trauma continues for a further 100 words and contains no referential or deictic link with the narrative or the characters of the novel. The next paragraph begins: 'To Dorothea, still in that

time of youth when the eyes with their long full lashes look out
after their rain of tears unsoiled and unwearied as a freshly-opened
passion-flower, that morning's parting with Will Ladislaw . . . '.
The key phrase is 'that time of youth'. It could refer back to the
generalization of the opening paragraph or be linked to the
particulars of Dorothea's age and her parting with Ladislaw.
There is no necessary structural 'tie' or cohesive link between the
two paragraphs, but for the reader the aphoristic observations
of the first become interfused with the narrative particulars of the
second. MacCabe (1978: 15) describes such juxtapositions and
mergers as follows: 'The metalanguage [of the first paragraph]
refuses to acknowledge its own status as writing – as marks of
material difference distributed through time and space.' In short,
it mediates universals of thought and behaviour in a way that
seems unaffected by particulars of circumstance or immediate
context. 'This unwritten text can then attempt to staunch the
haemorrhage of interpretations threatened by the material of
language' (ibid.: 18). It offers a framework of moral and philosophic norms into which the reader is invited, perhaps obliged, to
fit actualities such as previous dialogues between Dorothea and
Ladislaw.

Emily Brontë's *Wuthering Heights* is very different in stylistic
and structural character from Eliot's *Middlemarch*, but it achieves
the similar effect of creating a metatext, a narrative structure, that
absorbs the untidy details of real-world discourse into the textual
structures of the novel. *Wuthering Heights* is an impressive exercise
in pushing the conventions of implied author, narrative and
implied reader to, at the time, their known limits.

There are at least six levels of interaction between addresser and
addressee in this novel: (1) Emily Brontë (actual author, creator of
text) addresses you or me (actual reader, text in hand); (2) we, as
implied readers, are drawn into the fictional-real world of Mr
Lockwood whose journal constitutes the substance of the text
(in MacCabe's terms the metatext); (3) Mr Lockwood, however,

discloses no desire or intention to tell anyone other than himself about the content of his personal diary. He is both addresser and addressee of this discourse; (4) Mr Lockwood was also the addressee of one Nellie Dean, whose narration of key events enables him to transcribe them as diary entries; (5) Nellie Dean is variously addresser, co-ordinator and participant in the narrative. How does Mr Lockwood know she is telling the truth?; (6) the participants of the narrative, which also include Catherine and Heathcliff, are at once addressers and addressees in the dialogic exchanges of the text.

The question of why Brontë chose such a complex pattern of textual levels could be related to her status as a woman and as a writer in mid-nineteenth-century England. Lockwood operates as both the guarantee of fictive realism and as the means by which Brontë, in MacCabe's terms, can 'staunch the haemorrhage of interpretations threatened by the material of language'. Catherine and Heathcliff are, it is implied, archetypes of unlicensed sexuality. A novel that disclosed the actualities of their words and thoughts by employing the kind of open focalization used by Fielding or Sterne could not have been published in the mid-nineteenth century. A female novelist who disclosed an implied experience of such 'material' would certainly not have found a publisher, and the dense, refractory structure of the narrative is a stylistic counterpart to Brontë's decision to disguise herself with the asexual pseudonym of 'Ellis Bell'.

10

ROMANTICISM

Romanticism following Augustanism was the second great upheaval in the history of post-Renaissance English poetry. Its manifesto was the Preface (1800) to the *Lyrical Ballads* (1798) in which Wordsworth made a number of radical claims regarding the nature and function of poetry. He stated that 'there neither is, nor can be, any *essential* difference between the language of prose and metrical composition'. He did not mean that there should be no stylistic difference between poetry and prose: indeed it could be claimed that the metrical and stylistic variety of Romantic verse emphasized rather than clouded this difference. He meant that, especially during the Augustan period, poetic language had become largely predictable, both in stylistic terms (dominated as it was by the closed couplet) and in terms of the issues, topics and frames of reference of poetic discourse. In 1798 prose was the vehicle for the exploration of the new philosophies of the Enlightenment and the new freedoms of the age of revolution. The novel, with its ability to absorb the complexities of non-literary discourses, had stolen the march on poetry as an aesthetic means of articulating, in Wordsworth's terms, 'the real language of men' and accommodating the 'spontaneous overflow of powerful feelings'.

Wordsworth faced the problem of how to alter the established function or subject of poetry while maintaining its uniqueness as a stylistic genre with its own capabilities. In the *Lyrical Ballads* he achieved this by drawing upon a genre that was demonstrably poetic but associated with low culture: the ballad. Mayo (1954) discusses the debt of the *Lyrical Ballads* to the sub-genre of the popular magazine ballad, which entertained the educated reader with sordid tales of incest, murder and rural weirdness. Wordsworth himself valued the form as a bridge between popular verse – in which issues of immediate relevance would be addressed by the balladeer – and the discourses of mainstream poetry. The vocabulary of Wordsworth's speakers and the reported speech of their subjects differ radically from the authoritative wit of Pope or Dryden: the teller of 'The Idiot Boy' uses such locutions as 'mighty fret', 'fiddle faddle', 'thoughts torment her sore' and 'Fond lovers yet not quite hob nob', without a hint of self-consciousness or irony. Such usages would qualify for Halliday's (1978) category of literary 'anti-language', 'the extreme case of social dialect', and Roger Fowler (1981:150) offers a revised definition of the literary uses of anti-language. It is 'a medium of negotiation between two communities, a transaction through which conflicts of ideology and identity are actively waged . . . a dialogue between ideologies, reflected in linguistic transformations'.

Fowler's subject is the novel: specifically the incorporation of the dialect and discourse of a social and criminal underclass in Anthony Burgess's *A Clockwork Orange* and William Burroughs's *Naked Lunch*. A comparable transaction and conflict between ideology and identity is achieved by Wordsworth in the *Lyrical Ballads*. Compare the following extracts from two of the poems in the collection, the first from 'The Idiot Boy', the second from 'Tintern Abbey':

And thus, to Betty's question, he
Made answer, like a traveller bold,
(His very words I give to you,)
'The cocks did crow to-whoo, to-whoo,
'And the sun did shine so cold'.
– Thus answered Johnny in his glory,
And that was all his travel's story.

                    If this
Be but a vain belief, yet, oh! how oft,
In darkness, and amid the many shapes
Of joyless day-light; when the fretful stir
Unprofitable, and the fever of the world,
Have hung upon the beatings of my heart,
How oft, in spirit, have I turned to thee,
O sylvan Wye!

If we submit these passages to Jakobson's diagram of the communicative circuit (p. 41) we can trace a number of similarities and differences.

Jakobson's diagram is a methodical survey of the stylistic and linguistic clues that enables critics such as Fowler to recognize 'conflicts between ideology and identity'. Jakobson's concepts of context, contact, phatic, code, message and the poetic function involve for the reader points of recognition. The message communicated by a linguistic act is enveloped in a network of socio-cultural registers. A phatic utterance (indicating uncertainty, hesitation, informality) in improvised speech between friends will establish a code of delivery which is very different from that used in the composition of an official letter. The message might be the same, but it is effectively altered by the linguistic-stylistic clues that tell us about the situation of its delivery and about the socio-cultural relationship between addresser and addressee. These clues are just as relevant to poems as to non-literary exchanges. The poem will draw upon a variety of literary and non-literary registers and these will carry social and cultural resonances. In Wordsworth's poems the poetic function encloses and influences their context and message, but in different ways. The stylistic character of 'The Idiot Boy' is associated with the social class of its practitioners and subjects: the tale told in the Inn by a narrator who is not embarrassed by the rhyming interface between his own contact signal ('I give to you') and the childlike chorus of Johnny ('to-whoo, to-whoo'). The non-dramatic blank verse of 'Tintern Abbey' encodes a very different pattern of conventions and associations, including Milton's Christian epic, *Paradise Lost*, and the high-cultural tradition of landscape poems by, amongst others, James Thomson and William Cowper: the elegant syntactic reversal at the line ending, 'the fretful stir/Unprofitable' is just as clear a signal of this poem's cultural associations and heritage as the ballad's 'to you – to-whoo'.

Consult Jakobson's diagram and you will find that Wordsworth is playing a subtle game with a poem's ability to construct an image of its addresser and addressee. The phatic elements and contact code of the ballad suggest an addresser who is at home with the primitive culture of the poem's characters – a world very different from that of the addresser who shares a stylistic frame-work with Milton. But 'The Idiot Boy', along with the other poems in the collection in ballad form, is not a predictable survey of rural backwardness and charm, something that might merely entertain a high-cultural addressee. It engages with universal issues of innate wisdom and justice that the addressee would usually associate with the high-cultural registers of blank verse.

Genette in *Figures of Literary Discourse* (1982; repr. in Lodge, 1988) discusses the political and social forces that underpin alter-ations in the established relation between style and function. Genette considers the complex mutual relationship between the synchronic and diachronic axes of literary history, noting that this can be altered by individual acts of genre-switching. 'Pushkin imported into great poetry the effects of eighteenth century album verse, Nekrassov borrowed from journalism and Vaudeville, Blok from gypsy songs, Dostoevsky from the detective novel'. Each was a significant moment in Russian literary history, but none involved the invention of a new stylistic form. Instead the relationship between stylistic codes (particularly those of high and low culture) in a given synchronic axis or period was altered, and this had an effect on the diachronic or historical progression of literary forms.

Wordsworth's experiment with the rural ballad did not promote the form into the currency of Romantic and post-Romantic verse, but it did have a significant effect on nineteenth-century poetic writing. The rural ballad was a narrative form with a number of similarities to the eighteenth-century novel. Like Fielding's fiction it trod a very narrow path between a predetermined structural shape and immediate events which appeared to affect the disposition and control of the addresser/narrator. The Romantic ode shares these characteristics. The addresser of odes by Wordsworth, Coleridge, Keats and Shelley employs the high-cultural registers of the educated poet, but shares with the addresser of the ballad a sense of unpredictable immediacy. In Keats's best-known odes ('To Psyche', 'To a Nightingale', 'On a Grecian Urn', 'On Melancholy') a very complex stanzaic structure is juxtaposed with the present-tense deictics of mental and perceptual exploration. One could argue that Wordsworth's use of the ballad re-established a feature of mainstream English poetry that had been lost in the shift from Renaissance to Augustan style. Donne's 'The Flea' and 'The Relic' involved a palpable tension between immediacy and poetic form that resurfaces both in the ballad and in the Romantic ode. The nineteenth-century dramatic monologue, dominated by Browning, could also claim an inheritance from Wordsworth's use of the ballad. Browning's addressers exist in a high-cultural continuum, but they maintain the fiction of formal structure as a function of circumstantial conditions.

The Romantic poet who employs a mode of genre-switching

even more radical than Wordsworth's is William Blake. In *Songs of Innocence and Experience* (1789 and 1794) Blake, like Wordsworth in the *Lyrical Ballads*, draws upon a low-cultural stylistic register – in this case the short-line ballad forms used to educate children in Christian codes and morality. Blake introduces into familiar, even domestic, stylistic forms an interface between (in Jakobson's terms) the syntagmatic and paradigmatic axes that was unprecedented in poetic writing. The following is 'London' from *Songs of Experience*:

> I wander thro' each charter'd street,
> Near where the charter'd Thames does flow,
> And mark in every face I meet
> Marks of weakness, marks of woe.
>
> In every cry of every Man,
> In every Infant's cry of fear,
> In every voice, in every ban,
> The mind-forg'd manacles I hear.
>
> How the Chimney-sweeper's cry
> Every black'ning Church appalls;
> And the hapless Soldier's sigh
> Runs in blood down Palace walls.
>
> But most thro' midnight streets I hear
> How the youthful Harlot's curse
> Blasts the new born Infant's tear,
> And blights with plagues the Marriage hearse.

In the first stanza the verbal emphasis is visual – the speaker 'marks' the 'marks', or, roughly translated, he visually apprehends evidence of weakness and woe. In the second stanza the visual is superseded by the auditory – he 'hears' a 'cry' and voices. In stanzas 3 and 4 any stability between these two verbal and perceptual conditions is subverted. How can the speaker 'hear' how every church is appalled by the chimney-sweeper's cry ('appalls' in both its modern figurative usage and its original spatial designation of draping with a pall)? And although a sigh can be heard, it is curious to find that its visual, metaphoric transformation into blood on palace walls is still governed by the auditory verb phrase. Even more confusing is the harlot's curse which is 'heard' to 'Blast' the 'Infant's tear' and 'blight' ('with plagues') 'the Marriage hearse'.

We could interpret these verbal and referential disruptions by investigating the functional register of the poem, by explaining its stylistic character in terms of its predicated context. Perhaps the verbal instability of the speaker's account is a token of the effect of his perceptions upon his ability to vocalize them. This sense of the speaker's intellectual and ratiocinative faculties in a state of disorder becomes even more apparent in his shifts between the particulars of his account and a more general frame of reference incorporating the horrors and injustices of late eighteenth-century England. 'Mark' could refer simply to the appearance of the Londoners or it could involve some reference to the biblical 'mark' of Cain or the 'mark' borne by the victimized and downtrodden inhabitants of Jerusalem (Ezekiel 9:4). 'Charter'd' could mean both the 'charter'd rights of Englishmen', a much used counter-blast to the repressive regime of the prime minister William Pitt, and could also refer to the immediate urban landscape, including the Thames, as literally 'charted', owned, confined, mapped out, designated for commercial use. 'Ban' could mean an element of repressive legislation or it could refer to the specific and agreed prohibitions of a specific marriage announcement. Throughout the poem the speaker shifts between the particulars of his account and echoes of a more universal fabric of discourses, and this effect is supplemented by the repetitive use of 'every'. Its first usage links it with the situation of the utterance, 'every face I meet', but its attachment to 'every Man', 'every Infant', 'every voice', 'every black'ning Church' sets up a tension between a universalized

frame of reference and the equally prominent definite article:
'*the* Chimney sweeper', '*the* hapless Soldier', *the* youthful Harlot',
the newborn Infant', '*the* Marriage hearse'. Are these individual
instances of the speaker's reported experience or is 'the' substituted
for the generic predeterminer 'all' or 'every'?

Keeping in mind the functional register of the text we can claim
that its stylistic and referential imbalances are unprecedented
in literary history. Even in the Renaissance lyric the sense of
pragmatic immediacy and mimesis does not reach the level of dis-
orientation, the unfocused almost surreal combination of events
and thoughts, achieved by Blake.

At the junction between the closing and opening lines of stanzas
2 and 3 we encounter an example of enjambment which creates
two separate deep structures within the same syntactic unit. The
verb phrase 'I hear' is vital both for the syntactic structure of stanza
2 and for that of stanza 3 (the full stop is absent in the original
edition). This creates a tension between the functional register, in
which the grammatical deviation could be explained as parataxis
(structure determined by the impassioned nature of the speech
act), and a type of textual foregrounding made available only by
the particular stylistic features of poetry – in this case the tension
between the stanzaic and syntactic elements.

Jakobson defined the poetic function as that which projects the
axis of selection into the axis of combination. Blake unsettles any
predictable balance between the two axes by causing the selective
axis to shift constantly between the particulars of urban life and
their moral and religious co-ordinates. But these shocking, almost
surreal effects are anchored to an established formal structure.
Blake is a more radical stylist than Wordsworth, but both achieve
their innovative effects by using familiar formal structures in
unusual ways. The modernists began to move away from this
model of retrospective switching. They began to both reject and
reshape the formal anchors of literary tradition.

11

MODERNISM AND NATURALIZATION

Modernist writing explores the limits of the double pattern. The poles of this pattern can be represented in two columns:

Poetic function	Referential function (Jakobson)
Conventional register	Cognitive register (Levin)
Literary language	Functional language
Diachronic axis	Synchronic axis.

Imbalances between these poles occur in pre-modernist writing: the eighteenth-century novel struggled to incorporate functional, non-literary styles within a single generic structure; Romantic poetics deliberately unsettled a routine and familiar balance between the conventional and cognitive registers. Modernism, however, involves much more radical shifts towards the left- or right-hand columns and unprecedented combinations of the two.

Sometimes the entire text will foreground the right-hand column and minimize the interference of the left. This is most common in the early free verse of the Imagists and I shall use William Carlos Williams's 'Spring and All' as an example. Less frequently an entire text will reverse this imbalance and maintain a self-conscious allegiance to the left-hand column. Joyce's *Finnegans Wake* (1939) is the archetype of this method. More frequent is the text which consistently unsettles any clear relationship between the two poles. T. S. Eliot's 'The Love Song of J. Alfred Prufrock' mixes conventional poetic devices with linguistic patterns that have more in common with interior monologue than with poetry. Joyce's *Ulysses* (1922) mixes non-literary styles with familiar and innovative literary models.

The following is William Carlos Williams's 'Spring and All' (1923):

By the road to the contagious hospital
under the surge of the blue
mottled clouds driven from the
northeast – a cold wind. Beyond the
waste of broad, muddy fields
brown with dried weeds, standing and fallen

patches of standing water
the scattering of tall trees

All along the road the reddish
purplish, forked, upstanding, twiggy
stuff of bushes and small trees
with dead, brown leaves under them
leafless vines –

Lifeless in appearance, sluggish,
dazed spring approaches –

How do we distinguish between, in Levin's terms, the cognitive and the conventional features of this poem? The latter are very thin on the ground. There are no figures or metaphors. It does not 'project the principle of equivalence from the axis of selection into the axis of combination'. The only mildly metaphoric use of the selective axis is the use of the adverb 'dazed' in relation to the non-human entity of 'spring' and this is a usage that would not be unusual in a letter or in conversation. There is no metrical stucture and no rhyme scheme. The poem is divided into lines, but the lines do not conform to any predictable length or rhythm.

The syntactic structure of Williams's text bears a close resemblance to that of Herbert's 'Prayer I'. The only predicate verb is the last word, 'approaches'. The rest of the poem is made up of auxiliary verb phrases, which prompts the reader to speculate on whether a more dominant verb phrase has been left out. If Williams had written 'I am standing on . . . ' or 'I am looking down . . . the road to the contagious hospital', the subsequent catalogue of impressions would have a more certain locative and syntactic grounding. What we have is, like Herbert's poem, an apparent example of parataxis: language organized at the moment of experience or perception without too much attention given to formal syntax. Unlike Herbert's sonnet, Williams's free verse text offers no tight metrical counterpoint to its syntactic disorder. Herbert's sonnet effectively organizes and structures its syntax, while Williams's lines appear to follow no predictable pattern. However, there is a number of examples of enjambed syntax, which suggests that the line structure is not a random pattern, and which creates effects that are unique to the poetic function of language.

The line ending at 'blue' could be a complete syntactic unit, with blue operating as a metonymic substitute for sky: but the syntax continues into 'blue mottled clouds' and re-engages 'blue' in its more familiar adjectival role. This is an example of what John Hollander (1975) calls contre-rejet, the use of the line to create two divergent and irreconcilable syntactic deep structures, and we have already encountered an instance of it in Blake's 'London'. This type of syntactic double-take becomes the stylistic keynote of Williams's poem.

The line structure is not governed by arbitrary laws of metre and rhyme. The relation between the syntax and the lines offers a mimetic representation of the relation between pre-linguistic perception and the representational speech act. Examples of form as a facsimile of hesitation occur at the lines ending with the definite article 'the': the completed line and the incomplete sentence represent the temporal gap between visual or mental perception and its linguistic counterpart. More complex and more patently contrived examples of this effect occur when the line and the sentence appear to be complete before being extended and revised (as with 'blue/mottled clouds'), leaving us with two deep structures enclosed within the same syntactic sequence: a formal representation of the dynamics of perception, thought and language. The most complex consists of the lines,

> small trees
> with dead, brown leaves under them
> leafless vines –

The phrase 'leafless vines' could be an economic summation of the preceding description: 'small trees with dead brown leaves under them. (They are) leafless vines.' Alternatively the whole sequence could be a continuous syntactic unit, with 'them leafless vines' as an example of informal demotic usage.

Clearly Williams's poem shifts the balance between the poetic and non-poetic registers of language far closer to the latter than any of the pre-modernist poems that we have looked at so far. However, he maintains a number of stylistic parallels with these texts. As with Donne's 'The Relic' and Blake's 'London', Williams's 'Spring and All' uses the tension between syntax and the line to foreground a tension between the functional, context-governed register of language and its counterpart in the more contrived, arbitrary structures of literary style.

Williams's poem is an example of the kind of modernist text where principal allegiance is given to the right-hand column of the double pattern. Joyce's *Ulysses* shows how any clear relationship between the two poles can be continuously unsettled. We have already considered an extract from *Ulysses* in which Molly Bloom's interior monologue combines inner and outer focalization, thought and language (p. 68). The objective and the method of interior monologue are comparable with those of Williams's poem: both break down the established stylistic conventions of their genres in order to negotiate a new, more realistic balance between representation and reality. However, *Ulysses* does not consist exclusively of interior monologue. The text shifts unpredictably between the inner speech of Bloom, Molly and Stephen, more objective narrational methods, journalistic reportage, a potted history of English prose style, operatic collage and theatrical dialogue. The following four passages relate details of the thoughts and activities of Leopold Bloom.

> He entered Davy Byrne's. Moral pub. He doesn't chat. Stands a drink now and then. But in leapyear once in four. Cashed a cheque for me once.
>
> What will I take now? He drew his watch.

> Bloom mur: best references. But Henry wrote it: it will excite me. You know now. In haste. Henry. Greek ee. Better add postscript. What is he playing now. In haste.

> BLOOM: (*Behind his hand*) She's drunk. The woman is inebriated. (*He murmers vaguely the past of Ephraim*) Shitbroleeth.

> What caused him irritation in his sitting posture? Inhibitory pressure of collar (size 17) and waistcoat (5 buttons), two articles of clothing superfluous in the costume of mature males and inelastic to alterations of mass by expansion.

Individually the passages establish their own stylistic character. The first is a combination of reporting clauses ('He enter . . .') and free indirect style ('Moral pub'). The second abandons concessions to external narrative for a more jumbled catalogue of Bloom's thoughts and reflections. The third switches genre from fiction to drama. The fourth moves away from literary style to a kind of pseudo-scientific objectivism, uncluttered by any generic associations or stylistic refractions.

Novels before *Ulysses* had filtered the narrative through a variety of narrational points of view, as in Emily Brontë's *Wuthering Heights*, but none had incorporated so many diverse and apparently unrelated stylistic and generic modes as are found in Joyce's text. The traditional novel maintains a consistent balance between narrational method and narrative, and this variously affects localized elements such as reported speech and broader notions of timescale and point of view. *Ulysses*, however, seems determined never to come to rest upon a single, persistent method of balancing the method of narration against the events narrated. It could be argued that Joyce's objective is to create a text which is realistic not only in terms of establishing the plausibility of the setting, the characters and their actions (this is a routine function of the novel) but also in its incorporation of practically every known method of linguistic mediation, literary and non-literary. Colin MacCabe follows this argument in his comparative study of nineteenth-century classic realism and the works of Joyce. We might recall that MacCabe accused the nineteenth-century novelist, particularly George Eliot, of 'repressing the operations of the signifier by positioning a metalanguage which exists outside of materiality and production' (1978: 36). *Ulysses* continually subverts any attempt by a reliable narrator to control the text and instead offers the reader a kaleidoscopic medley of linguistic forms. David Lodge (1981) sums up the effect of this: 'The reader of *Ulysses* is never allowed to sink into the comfortable assurance of an interpretation guaranteed by the narrator, but must himself produce the meaning of the text by opening himself fully to the play of its diverse and contradictory discourses.' What is absent from the novel is any secure or persistent narrational meta-language.

The two types of modernist style created by Williams and Joyce offer different perspectives on a single question. What is the relationship between literature and the non-literary sphere of discourses and events generally known as reality? Both attempt to make the relationship more intimate. In Williams's poem the literary and non-literary registers of the text are elided in a way that creates an impression of immediacy and unforced spontaneity. In Joyce's novel the processes of literary composition and narrative structuring are incessantly foregrounded, contrasted and explored. Williams posits a model of literary imitation in which the structures and stylistic registers of the text are responsive to their perceptual and ratiocinative origins. Joyce posits an opposing model in which this hierarchy is reversed: in *Ulysses* the ceaseless alterations in the manner, style and function of linguistic mediation represent, at least in MacCabe's view, reality as collage of discourses, the real world as a construct of whatever linguistic shape we choose or are obliged to give it.

Williams subdues and modulates the purely poetic register of the text while Joyce foregrounds the uneasy relation between fiction and non-literary discourse. T. S. Eliot's 'The Love Song of J. Alfred Prufrock' (1917) is similar to Joyce's text in that it both draws upon and unsettles the relation between poetic and non-poetic discourses.

> And the afternoon, the evening, sleeps so peacefully!
> Smoothed by long fingers,
> Asleep . . . tired . . . or it malingers,
> Stretched on the floor, here beside you and me.
> Should I, after tea and cakes and ices,
> Have the strength to force the moment to its crisis?
> But though I have wept and fasted, wept and prayed

But though I have seen my head (grown slightly bald)
  brought in upon a platter,
I am no prophet – and here's no great matter;
I have seen the moment of my greatness flicker,
And I have seen the eternal Footman hold my coat, and
  snicker,
And in short, I was afraid.

(lines 75–86)

As with Donne's 'The Relic', we can first use the deictic features of the text to identify a speaker with recognizable thoughts and ideas. However, although the first-person pronoun is a relatively stable and consistent feature of the text, it resists our attempts to construct a clearly defined speaking presence and a contextual situation for the utterance.

Who exactly is the 'you' referred to in line 78? It might well be the person invited by the speaker in the first line of the poem to accompany him on a strange journey: 'Let us go then, you and I'. But we are never certain if the journey is an account of places visited and people met, or a mental progress through half-remembered events, anxieties and literary-biblical quotations. When the speaker asks: 'Have [I] the strength to force the moment to its crisis?' we face a similarly inconclusive tension between concrete and abstract registers of meaning. Does this crucial moment have something to do with the 'overwhelming question' that seems to underpin the speaker's social and intellectual excursions? Or is the 'moment' in some way connected with the relationship between 'you and me', suggesting that the 'you' is not the putative reader but an acquaintance of the speaker (a friend, lover or alter ego?) His later reference to 'some talk of you and me' (line 89) implies that the 'you' is part of the fictive world of the poem.

The procedures through which Donne created a tension between text and context were clear and specific: the pristine stanzaic formula jarred against the emotionally charged immediacy of the speaker's account. In Donne's poem the paraphrased version of the speaker's circumstances and problems could be compared with a non-literary situation. If the discourse were not embedded in the stanzaic form it might easily have occurred in a journal or an intimate conversation. Eliot makes it much more difficult for the reader to disentangle the conflicting formal and referential registers. Even without Eliot's metrical undertow and irregular rhyme scheme, the monologue is bizarre and discontinuous. Throughout the poem the speaker shifts unpredictably between immediate locative references ('here beside you and me . . . after tea and cakes and ices') and a broader frame of reference in which he draws upon citations from classical and Renaissance literature, the Bible and philosophy, alongside allusions to the social and domestic conventions of society *circa* 1917. Citing the methods of pragmatics and sociolinguistics we might claim that the discourse consists of relaxed, informal speech forms (the hesitations of line 77, the demotic register of 'my head (grown slightly bald)', 'no great matter', 'snicker') which in turn suggest a degree of non-literary improvisation on the part of the speaker. At the same time this pattern becomes an element of the patently literary structure: 'ices' rhymes comically with 'crisis'. The self-mocking juxtapositions of domestic and personal detail with universal themes (his own head 'grown slightly bald' interposed with the myth of Salome and John the Baptist, for instance) are enclosed within a disturbingly solemn couplet.

> But though I have wept and fasted, wept and prayed (line 81) . . .
> And in short, I was afraid. (line 86)

In most regular, pre-modernist poems the relationship between the purely poetic and the intergeneric registers of the text operates at agreed levels of contrast and difference. The Augustan couplet employs metre and rhyme as structural underpinnings for the controlled parallelism of the syntax. Blake's *Songs* maintain a degree of contrast between the singsong domesticity of the ballad form and the provocative, radical nature of the message. Eliot's method makes it difficult to differentiate between the poetic and the non-poetic elements of the text, and in this respect there are similarities between 'Prufrock', 'Spring and All' and *Ulysses*. All three unbalance the established, pre-modernist configurations of literary and non-literary registers.

Modernism is important for stylistics mainly because of the problems it presents for naturalization. Naturalization is a normative operation in which the strange, the formal and the fictional are rendered familiar to us. When we naturalize a text we return it to the discursive framework of ordinary language that it seeks to disrupt. A crucial element in this is our ability to distinguish between the literary and non-literary elements of the text. This grants us a secure perspective on the methods employed by the text to defamiliarize ordinary language and refract familiar subjects and ideas.

The following are two very different models of naturalization, by Menakhem Perry and Roland Barthes:

> any reading of a text is a process of constructing a system of hypotheses or frames which can create maximal relevancy among the various data of the text – which can motivate their 'co-presence' in the text according to models derived from 'reality', from literary or cultural conventions, and the like.
>
> (Perry, 1979: 43)

> the space of writing is to be ranged over, not pierced; writing ceaselessly posits meaning ceaselessly to evaporate it, carrying out a systematic exemption of meaning . . . a text is made of multiple writings, drawn from many cultures and entering into mutual relations of dialogue, parody, contestation . . . . The reader is the space on which all the quotations that make up a writing are inscribed without any of them being lost; a text's unity lies not in its origin but in its destination.
>
> (Barthes *Image – Music – Text*, 1977; repr. in Lodge, 1988: 171)

Perry invokes the procedures of stylistics as a means of stabilizing the relation between what happens in a text and perceived reality: we document and stratify its various details in relation to models derived from non-literary reality and from literary-cultural conventions. Barthes argues that the multiplicity of stylistic and referential overlaps constantly resists our attempts to carry out an objective empirical analysis of how a text works and what it means: any form of unity or posited meaning resides in the individual reader's impression.

In a general sense Perry and Barthes represent, respectively, textualist and reader-centred contextualist approaches to style and criticism. But rather than classify their approaches as simply a result of literary-critical disagreement it would be useful to test their validity against our experience of modernist style.

Joyce's *Finnegans Wake* (1939) is the archetype and extremity of modernist writing. It invokes and unsettles practically every stylistic convention of literature. *Finnegans Wake* is generally perceived to be a novel, but it is extremely difficult to make any of it conform to the structural frameworks that define the genre. There is a narrator, but this presence is defined not in terms of his/her control of focalizing angles, descriptive methods, use of time and space or deployment of reported speech: rather, the narrator is the style of the entire text. Moreover the style is without precedent in literary and non-literary discourses. It is poetic in that it constantly unsettles familiar, lexical and referential patterns with portmanteau words which connote geographical, mythical, literary and historical registers, and it supplements this with extra-syntactic sequences of assonance and alliteration. It is difficult in 'Prufrock' to disentangle the literary from the non-literary registers; in *Finnegans Wake* it is impossible. No referential framework or deictic structure remains secure for long enough to establish itself as the background to a stylistic pattern.

There is some evidence to associate the narrator with a Mr Porter who might be giving an account of his dream, in which he takes on the role of a textual dreamself called Humphrey Chimpden Earwicker (whose initials frequently mutate into Here Comes Everybody or such specific, locative forms as Howth Castle and Environs). A key element in any stylistic analysis is the identification of a centralizing focus or perspective but in Joyce's text this putative presence is effectively absorbed into the continuously shifting stylistic fabric. The following is an extract from the second paragraph of page 1:

> Sir Tristram violer d'amores fr'over the short sea, had passencore re-arrived from North America on this side the scraggy isthmus of Europe Minor to wielderfight his penisolate war . . .

It is impossible to find a framework of broad narrative structuring that will allow us to specify in Perry's terms the 'various data of the text', and we might attempt with this extract to identify a more local stylistic register.

The extra-textual resonances are numerous and multilayered. Sir Tristram carries allusions to Tristram Shandy (hero of another experimental novel) and Tristan of Tristan and Isolde, both of whom are referred to elsewhere in this part of the book; 'violer d'amores' connotes both the notion of sexual violation and the viola, both again invoking regular allusions. 'Passencore' echoes passenger and the French *pas encore* (not yet): Sir Tristram might be accompanied on his journey, or about to arrive. 'Wielderfight' could be a portmanteau, demotic pronunciation of 'will the fight' or 'wield the fight', or possibly a corrupt Anglo-German notion of 'fight again' (German *wieder* = again), the 'penisolate war' could refer to a conflict involving the penis, the pen, or occurring on the peninsula.

The extract seems to satisfy Jakobson's definition of the poetic function, which 'projects the principle of equivalence from the axis of selection into the axis of combination'. The selective axis is never at rest. Joyce is always inventing unusual lexical and semantic constructions (connoting a vast framework of references) which will react with other equally unexpected projections along the syntagmatic, combinative chain. In fact, the syntagmatic deep structure is the only stable element of the book. In the passage quoted the ambiguities occur predominantly within the noun phrases and qualifying clauses. The main verbs establish clearly enough that Sir Tristram is moving from North America to Europe. There is a close similarity between Joyce's use of a syntactic deep structure as the basis for multiple, alternative meanings and the poetic double pattern. However as we have already seen, Riffaterre has pointed out that such a multilayered fabric in a sonnet would overload the cognitive faculties of the reader. If it requires a 'super-reader' to simultaneously apprehend, let alone naturalize, the formal and referential complexities of fourteen iambic lines, what kind of being would be able to follow the same textual densities for 500 pages? *Finnegans Wake* is, as Barthes claims, a 'space of writing to be ranged over, not pierced; [it] ceaselessly posits meaning, ceaselessly to evaporate it, carrying out a systematic exemption of meaning' (Lodge, 1988:171). It is impossible, in Perry's terms, to find 'a system of hypotheses of frames which can create maximal relevancy among the various data of the text' (1979: 43). All of the known systems and frames of stylistic analysis – focalization, grammars of narrative, Jakobsonian poetics – are effectively dismantled by the text's endless interweavings of device and meaning.

Barthes's model of naturalization – or rather the impossibility of objective naturalization – is valid for *Finnegans Wake*, but Perry's model is applicable to the vast majority of conventional texts and indeed for many works – such as our other examples from Joyce, Williams and Eliot – in the modernist mainstream. The opposition of the two models provides us with an intriguing perspective on the progress and quite possibly the terminus of literary history.

In *Finnegans Wake* the only recognizable feature that the text shares with non-literary discourse is the syntagmatic deep structure.

The rest is a dense saturation of semantic parallelism, referential echoes and unresolvable ambiguities: the literary dimension almost displaces its non-literary counterpart. Verse such as Williams's shifts the balance in the opposite direction: its recognizably poetic features subtly shadow and deflect the predominantly non-literary, improvisational structure of the text.

To shift the balance any further in either direction would be to destroy the double pattern. A text without Williams's elegantly slight counterpoints of syntax and poetic form would no longer be recognizable as a poem. A dense, multilayered text which removed Joyce's structural core of the syntagm would be completely incomprehensible, in literary or non-literary terms. In the former case Perry's system of frameworks which links the literary text to its non-literary counterparts would be unnecessary because there would be no differences. In the latter, Barthes's concept of the reader as the 'destination' of meaning would be invalid, because there would be no concessions to meaning.

Modernism is effectively the terminus of literary history, by which I mean that the limits of the double pattern have now been established in literary texts. Before modernism the vast majority of literary writings worked within these limits. The eighteenth-century novel explored ways in which established non-literary styles and functions could be organized within the evolving structure of fictional narrative. The objective was to bring these features together, and the eventual result was the nineteenth-century classic realist novel. Two centuries of establishing balances and symmetries within the double pattern (with slight aberrations by the likes of Sterne) gave way in modernism to a culture which tested the relationship between literary and non-literary registers, from the informal transparencies of stream of consciousness to the dense, literary excesses of *Finnegans Wake*. Renaissance, Augustan and Romantic poets developed styles and habits which altered pre-established balances between referential and stylistic registers: the double pattern was the framework within which these shifts occurred, and only such notables as Blake and Walt Whitman went significantly beyond its limits. Modernist poetry began to test these boundaries. Williams perceived formal structures such as the line and metaphor as elements that should follow rather than coerce the expressive movement of the text. Eliot, conversely, allowed the formal and figurative character of 'Prufrock' to absorb and obscure its apparent meaning.

The terminus of literary history does not preclude further stylistic experimentation. B. S. Johnson's *The Unfortunates* (1969) is a 'novel' consisting of loose-leaf sheets which the reader can redistribute to produce his/her own narrative pattern: implied reader can occasionally take control of implied author, and again the boundaries of the fictional text have been reached. Richard Brautigan's *Trout Fishing in America* (1967) is the prose equivalent of Eliot's 'Prufrock' in that the stylistic indulgences and excesses of the narrator obscure any balance between *sjuzet* and *fabula*: the text is pure *sjuzet*, but unlike *Finnegans Wake* the style is self-consciously personal:

> The sun was like a huge fifty-cent piece that someone had poured kerosene on and then had lit with a match and said, 'Here, hold this while I go get a newspaper,' and put the coin in my hand, but never came back.
>
> ('Red Lip': 7–8)

Compare this with Eliot's metaphor involving the animal and the fog (above, p. 27). Similarly, the subject of Brautigan's simile (the sun) is effectively replaced by its figurative counterpart. Throughout the novel, any paraphrasable narrative of place, time and event (*fabula*) is lost in a proliferation of figurative excursions. Again the double pattern of traditional fiction, the tension between fictional modes and the text's relation to the non-fictional world, is replaced by style for its own sake.

There will no doubt be further experimental texts which explore the limits and range of the double pattern, but such explorations will always acknowledge these limitations. To go beyond them in either direction will mean that the text ceases to exist either as literature or as comprehensible language.

Literary styles can feature in non-literary discourses, and vice versa, but a literary text is defined by a tension between these two elements that permeates its entirety: modernism has shown how far this tension can be stretched.

PART III

GENDER AND EVALUATION

12

GENDER AND GENRE

The following is Andrew Marvell's 'To his Coy Mistress', a poem published in 1681, but thought to have been written in the 1650s.

Had we but World enough, and Time,
This coyness Lady were no crime.
We would sit down, and think which way
To walk, and pass our long Love's Day.
Thou by the *Indian Ganges* side
Should'st Rubies find: I by the Tide
Of *Humber* would complain. I would
Love you ten years before the Flood:
And you should if you please refuse
Till the Conversion of the *Jews*.
My vegetable Love should grow
Vaster than Empires, and more slow.
An hundred years should go to praise
Thine Eyes, and on thy Forehead Gaze.
Two hundred to adore each Breast:

But thirty thousand to the rest.
An Age at least to every part,
And the last Age should show your Heart.
For Lady you deserve this State;
Nor would I love at lower rate.
  But at my back I alwaies hear
Time's winged Charriot hurrying near:
And yonder all before us lye
Desarts of vast Eternity.
Thy Beauty shall no more be found;
Nor, in thy marble Vault, shall sound
My ecchoing Song: then Worms shall try
That long preserv'd Virginity:
And your quaint Honour turn to dust;
And into ashes all my Lust.
The Grave's a fine and private place,
But none I think do there embrace.
  Now therefore, while the youthful hew
Sits on thy skin like morning dew,
And while thy willing Soul transpires
At every pore with instant Fires,
Now let us sport us while we may;
And now, like am'rous birds of prey,
Rather at once our Time devour,
Than languish in his slow-chapt pow'r.
Let us roll all our Strength, and all
Our sweetness, up into one Ball:
And tear our Pleasures with rough strife,
Thorough the Iron gates of Life.
Thus, though we cannot make our Sun
Stand still, yet we will make him run.

To describe what happens when we read this poem we must consider the way in which its stylistic register affects its meaning.

It is written in octosyllabic couplets, and the relationship between metre, rhyme scheme and syntax is rather more relaxed and unpredictable than in the later couplet poems of the Restoration and eighteenth century. There is no continuous pattern that governs the relation between the structure of the couplet and the disposition of noun and verb phrases. The two syntactic units of lines 5–7 involve an identical framework of subject, object and verb, but these do not run parallel with the structure of each couplet:

> Thou by the *Indian Ganges* side
> Should'st rubies find: I by the Tide
> Of *Humber* would complain.

Throughout the poem there is a tension between two stylistic registers. The metrical pattern is a repetitive feature of the text which inscribes it within a tradition of literary conventions and practices. But the syntax pulls against this impersonal, arbitrary scheme, embodies the hesitations, thoughts and idiosyncrasies of a specific speaking voice and links the text with the non-literary sphere of discourse, dialogue and the exchange of information.

The opening lines suggest a condition of immediacy and improvisation; of an utterance generated by the particular experience of the addresser and addressee. The subject is '*this* coyness'; not the general problem of coyness or a particular memory or hypothesis, but the addressee's apparent reluctance to submit to the addresser's sexual advances at this moment. When we consider the rhetorical strategy of the addresser this sense of immediacy and urgency becomes even more apparent. The mood and the syntactic character of the first paragraph is conditional and speculative. The metaphoric excursions are fantastic: her body and his contemplation of it – both invoking the ephemeral, limited nature of mortal existence and sensual pleasure – are transformed into almost limitless expanses of space and time. The second paragraph maintains the extravagant metaphoric tone, but changes from the conditional to the specific and possessive mood: 'my back', 'before us lye', 'Thy beauty', 'your quaint Honour', 'my Lust'. The third paragraph confirms a much-debated feature of the text. Its organization into three premises follows the formula of the philosophical syllogism: there is this, and there is that; therefore there must be . . . . Again we find that the addresser combines a device drawn from the non-literary sphere of scholastic philosophy with a pattern of overtly poetic conventions.

So far I have emphasized the textual features that enable us to consider the effect of the poem and to construct a situation for the utterance. Let us now shift the emphasis further towards this imagined contextual situation. The addressee is undoubtedly female: how does this affect our status as critics and readers? So far, my observations about the stylistic devices of metre, metaphor, structural organization and deictic positioning have been impartial and objective, but it becomes difficult to maintain this approach when we consider the effects of these upon the addressee. The only mental or emotional attribute conceded to the addressee is her apparent inclination to coyness. Every other verbal, adjectival or nominal feature is physical. The pseudo-religious concept of purity and 'virginity' preserved beyond mortal existence is compromised by an image of physical violation: 'then Worms shall try/That long preserv'd virginity'. And the concept of her eternal 'honour' is similarly tainted by a familiar contemporary pun: 'quaint' was frequently substituted for 'cunt'. The addresser's ingenious rhetorical strategy, irrespective of its component devices, rests upon the assumption that the addressee is a person whose sense of identity is a function of her physical attractiveness. In the first paragraph the male speaker offers her the tantalizing possibility that this might be preserved beyond the normal span of human existence, and in the second he presents her with the disagreeable fact that it cannot. The entire text confirms and sustains the most extreme version of ascribed gender roles and it opens up a whole range of perspectives on the relation between literary style and the representation of gender.

Consider the following riddle:

> In a motorway accident a man is killed and his son severely injured. The boy is rushed to a casualty ward and the unit's most eminent specialist in the treatment of physical trauma is summoned. The surgeon arrives with a retinue of assistants, hesitates and explains, 'I can't operate on him. He's my son.'

Not all listeners find this puzzling, but many admit to a slight feeling of shock at the surgeon's disclosure. Prior to her statement, the surgeon is an ungendered subject, but many listeners admit that they naturalize this figure – eminent, active, dominant, involved in the stark physicality of life and death – as male.

Now let us consider what the writing of regular poetry requires. It involves the ability to coerce an unlimited range of linguistic and referential registers into an arbitrary pattern of metrical rules and conventions. The control exerted by Marvell's addresser over his linguistic material (and, it is implied, over his addressee) is explicitly related to maleness. But even if the topic and the addresser of a poem are ungendered (which is usually the case), intellectual control is a significant feature of the act of writing. Just as we frequently associate the role of the heroic figure who cuts, binds and repairs the human body with notions of maleness, so we might similarly assume that an anonymous presence who displays an aggressive, confident control of two linguistic registers is a man.

Virginia Woolf, in addressing the question of why there are more pre-twentieth-century women novelists than poets, claimed that 'the novel alone was young enough to be soft in [their] hands'. In short the eighteenth- and nineteenth-century novel was exploring and establishing its own stylistic conventions; it was 'young' enough to maintain a distance from a male-dominated cultural heritage. Gilbert and Gubar in *The Madwoman in the Attic* (1979) qualify this thesis with a practical consideration: women, if they were to write at all, would by the late eighteenth century have been more likely to generate a professional income from the sale of novels than from the publication of poems. But they also agree that women poets faced the intimidating prospect of participating in a stylistic field whose registers and cultural associations were predominantly male.

Gilbert and Gubar refer to the historically and theologically sanctioned association of 'the poetic passion' with mysterious inspiration, divine afflatus and bardic ritual – an aesthetic manifestation of the priesthood. 'But if in Western culture women cannot be priests, then how – since poets are priests – can they be poets?' (reprinted in M. Eagleton, 1986: 110). But the most influential determinant of the genre–gender relationship is stylistic:

> Finally, and perhaps most crucially, where the novel allows – even encourages – just the self-effacing withdrawal society has traditionally fostered in women, the lyric poem is in some sense the utterance of a strong, assertive 'I'. Artists from Shakespeare to Dickinson, Yeats and T. S. Eliot have of course qualified this 'I' emphasizing, as Eliot does, the 'extinction of personality' involved in a poet's construction of an artful masklike persona, or insisting, as Dickinson did, that the speaker of poems is a 'supposed person'. But, nevertheless, the central self that speaks or sings a poem must be forcefully defined, whether 'she' or 'he' is real or imaginary. If the novelist, therefore, inevitably sees herself from the *outside*, as an object, a character, a small figure in a large pattern, the lyric poet must be continually aware of herself from the inside, as a subject, a speaker: she must be, that is, assertive, authoritative, radiant with powerful feelings while at the same time absorbed in her own consciousness – and hence, by definition, profoundly 'unwomanly', even freakish.
>
> (ibid.: 111)

Gilbert and Gubar present us with a new and intriguing perspective on Jakobson's theory of the poetic function. Jakobson argues that there is a constant, irreconcilable ambiguity between the textual addresser and his/her contextually determined counterpart, but that they share the imperative of projecting the speaking voice into the impersonal network of poetic conventions and devices. Gilbert and Gubar show that this same act of projecting is an aesthetic manifestation of the traditionally prescribed role of the male in a variety of linguistic and social functions, a role that is 'profoundly "unwomanly"'.

Let us now consider how this concept of gender–genre relations relates to a number of issues already considered in our examination of stylistics and literary history. The part played by the woman in the seventeenth-century amatory lyric is straightforward. She might feature as a physical correlative for the deictic features of the text or as the inspiration for some of its metaphoric excursions. Inevitably she will remain silent. In drama, where the female addressee can answer back, her function is usually marginalized by an imposing complex of contextual elements. We noted that Isabella in *Measure for Measure* becomes more a functionary of the textual pattern than, like her male counterparts, an arbiter in the shifting relations between style and its referent. Her brief one-to-one exchange with Angelo in which they battle over the true meaning of that elusive signified, justice, is rapidly exchanged for her role as an exploitable and transformable signifier: the Duke, rather like Marvell's addresser, plays a textual game with her physical presence. A similar textual function is played out by Portia in *The Merchant of Venice* (1596–8). She operates as an active linguistic and physical presence only in the world of Belmont, a world safely detached from the unreliable signifiers of Venice. She does, of course, transform and reinterpret the plot and its moral-judicial underpinnings, but she does so as a man. One might even compliment Shakespeare for his prescient analogue of the woman writer in the eighteenth and nineteenth centuries: Belmont and Isabella's convent, as Gilbert and Gubar write of the novel, 'allows – even encourages – just the self-effacing withdrawal society has traditionally fostered in women'; while 'the utterance of a strong, assertive "I"' in the lyric poem or in society is left to the man in Venice, or the woman disguised as the man.

Sandra Gilbert in 'Patriarchal Poetry and Women Readers' (1978) discusses the immense power that Milton's *Paradise Lost* has exercised upon women readers and, consequently, women writers. Milton had effectively appropriated the originary archetype of male and female roles and reconstructed this as a literary text. One element of this monolithic influence that Gilbert only touches on is Milton's presentation of a causal relation between gender and genre. Throughout *Paradise Lost* Eve dutifully obeys the rules that would determine the function of women in the postlapsarian, Western, world. Adam functions as her adviser. She is never present during the lengthy dialogues between her partner and the advisory angel, Raphael. The wisdom of these exchanges is transmitted to her, later, by Adam. Her moment of independence, her chance to explore her much-vaunted gift of reason and, more significantly, to test the relation between language and the ultimate truth (i.e. What exactly is meant by the rule of obedience?), comes in her exchange with Satan. During this exchange she is partly persuaded and partly persuades herself that eating the fruit is part of God's hidden plan. The result of this, as Christianity continually reminds us, is the Fall.

Some years earlier, Milton had enacted a very similar exchange between 'The Lady' and the eponymous demon, Comus. And one suspects that the Lady's response to Comus is a thinly disguised sermon both to our universal mother and to her female descendants. Comus attempts to persuade her to have sex with him and he employs the strategies of wit and metaphoric play that feature in the amatory lyric. The lady replies:

> I had not thought to have unlocked my lips
> In this unhallowed air, but that this juggler
> Would think to charm my judgement, as mine eyes,
> Obtruding false rules pranked in reason's garb. . . .

Thou hast not ear nor soul to apprehend
The sublime notion and high mystery
That must be uttered to unfold the sage
And serious doctrine of Virginity . . . .

Enjoy your dear wit and gay rhetoric
That hath so well been taught her dazzling fence;
Thou art not fit to hear thyself convinced.

(*Comus*, 1634, lines 756–92)

Milton, through his character, is the spokesman for the silent (or in Shakespeare's case silenced) Lady of Renaissance literature. Poetry, Milton concedes, is 'false rules pranked in reason's garb'. It has nothing to do with the disclosure or the projection of such sublime notions and high mysteries as the serious doctrine (with half an eye on Isabella) of Virginity – and this passage looks forward to Eve's enthusiastic participation with Satan in an outright festival of reason-twisting and poetic double-dealing, their subject being the sublime notion of the will of God and the high mystery of the future of mankind.

There is a common thread running through all of these encounters between gender and genre, and it confirms the bizarre and paradoxical relation between poetry and the 'real world' reflected and enacted in non-literary discourses. On the one hand poetry, particularly during the Renaissance, is perceived as standing at the head of the aristocracy of literary and non-literary genres – and its use by Shakespeare as the medium in drama for the conditions of ambition, executive power, governance and existential responsibility confirms this association of authority with high art. Consequently, poetry, alongside the positions of authority and dominance that it supports and mediates, is considered to be an unwomanly activity. On the other hand, poetry is, as Milton suggests, capable of exposing and foregrounding the anarchic relationship between truth and fabrication, between the signified and its referent and the ungrounded signifier; capable of showing that the notions of moral, philosophic and religious certainty that underlie social structure are friable constructions of language. This is an activity thought to be too subversive, too dangerously liberating in its control of the signifier above the signified, to be appropriate to the prescribed roles and activities of women.

The following lines were written by Anne Finch, Countess of Winchilsea, probably the best-known woman poet of the late seventeenth and early eighteenth centuries. She addresses three male poets.

> Happy you three! Happy the Race of Men!
> Born to inform or to correct the Pen
> To proffitts pleasures freedom and command
> Whilst we beside you but as Cyphers stand
> T'increase your Numbers and to swell th'account
> Of your delights which from our charms amount
> And sadly are by this distinction taught
> That since the Fall (by our seducement wrought)
> Ours is the greater losse as ours the greater fault.

This passage operates at two levels. It is an informed, sardonic reflection upon the perceived relation between women and writing, and it confirms the argument that style can at once mediate and transform its referent. Finch comments on how women can feature as the subjects but not the producers of poetic discourse, a role established by the original part played by Eve.

Given that it was written in the mid-eighteenth century the style of the passage is radical and, in terms of the diachronic axis of stylistic regulation, disobedient. The closed couplet, an institution of eighteenth-century poetic style, is used by Finch as a means of disrupting rather than, in Popeian terms, sustaining and specifying the subject of the discourse. The couplets and lines ending at 'Pen' and 'stand' could close their syntactic units, but we are led forward into dependent sub-clauses. This device of 'contre-rejet' involves using the non-syntactic structure of the poetic line to cause an interpretive double-take: the syntax seems to have completed its specification of sense, yet moves forward to elaborate on the point already made. This sense of ambiguity is paralleled by the constant shifts in the semantic centre of gravity between three themes: the image of wealth and acquisition, the activity of writing and the act of sexual dominance. Each of the principal noun and verb phrases resonates with a semantic trace which unsettles its apparent, syntactically determined meaning. In the third line, for example, the word 'proffitts' carries forward a residual sense of the benefits of writing (to profit by informing or correcting the activities of the 'Pen'), a sense which will be transformed into a pattern of financial images: 'Cyphers', 'Numbers', 'swell th'account', 'amount'. The three conditions of 'pleasures freedom and command' are similarly dispersed through several subsequent semantic registers. There are the 'pleasures freedom and command' of writing about women, the 'cyphers' (subjects) of poems whose 'Numbers' (a contemporary term denoting measure and syllabic length) will as a consequence 'increase' and 'swell'. Carried along with this pattern are images of sexual pleasure, freedom and command: women are 'cyphers', child-bearers who increase the dynastic 'Numbers', and they are also the source of more straightforward sexual 'delights', an adverb surrounded by the phallic *double entendres* of 'increase', 'swell' and 'amount'.

The word which at once synthesizes and disrupts these various patterns of form and signification is 'Pen'. Feminist and non-feminist critics have often remarked, sometimes farcically, upon the drift between the semantic and contextual conditions of 'pen' and 'penis', and Finch would indeed seem to have created an intriguing interplay of text and context: it rhymes with men, it features as a vital instrument in the activities of financial gain and poetic endeavour; and its function in the pattern of sexual and procreative images seems clear enough.

Finch's stylistic achievements in this short passage are considerable. She creates a multilayered, polyphonic text, reminiscent of the radical interplay of form and signification in metaphysical verse, combining a method and an effect which ran against the dominant mood of Augustan writing. In an important sense she set a standard that would be followed by a large number of women writers.

Mary Jacobus (1979: 12) claims that in 'the [patriarchal] theoretical scheme, femininity itself – heterogeneity, Otherness – becomes the repressed term by which discourse is made possible. The feminine takes its place with the absence, silence or incoherence that discourse represses.' By 'the repressed term by which discourse is made possible' Jacobus means that the norms, conventions and habits that govern communication effectively appropriate femaleness as a subject. Women are of course allowed to participate in conversation, even to write, but since male expectations and perceptions determine the manner and function of speech and writing the woman becomes rather like a figure in a painting, a participatory element of the overall message but dispossessed of any active role in the formulation of the message. This role emerges clearly enough in the silencing, appropriation and marginalization of the female subject in the above examples from Shakespeare, Milton and Marvell. The Lady, despite her individuality and intelligence, can only counter Comus's discourse with silence. Both he and she know that if she were to enter the discourse she would become its subject, as did the similarly individualistic Isabella in the broader discourse of *Measure for Measure*. Finch escapes these conditions of 'absence, silence and incoherence' not by refusing to participate in the prescriptive codes of poetic discourse but by creating continuous parallels between her own self-conscious exploration of femaleness and her disruptions of the governing conventions of eighteenth-century poetic form. Finch's achievement is more clearly specified by Hélène Cixous (1981: 249, 258): 'A feminine text cannot fail to be more than subversive. It is volcanic . . . . If she's a her-she, it's in order to smash everything, to shatter the framework of institutions, to blow up the law, to shatter the "truth" with laughter.'

Jacobus contends that literary writing is complicit with the network of non-literary discourses in reflecting and maintaining the repressed condition of women in society. Cixous argues that the only strategy available to the woman writer is subversion and experiment, an unshackling of the literary code from its more deeply entrenched counterparts in non-literary discourse. A common feature of the work of many of the greatest women writers is a deliberate alteration of the familiar relationship between the two dimensions of the double pattern – those elements of the text which announce its stylistic allegiance to literary writing and those features which maintain its relationship with non-literary, referential discourse.

Finch's message contains, even in the eighteenth century, a very familiar complaint against the cultural patriarchy, but what distinguishes and strengthens her poetry is her ability to combine this paraphrasable element with a skilful and sardonic reworking of those stylistic conventions that constitute the predominantly male discourse of poetry.

An apparently very different, though in fact closely related, strategy occurs in the first literary sub-tradition to be substantially populated by women writers: the Gothic novel. Ann Radcliffe, Charlotte Dacre, Elizabeth Helme, Isabella Kelly, Mary Meake and Eleanor Sleath kept alive the Gothic tradition throughout the late eighteenth and early nineteenth centuries. In purely stylistic terms the Gothic novel was not a revolutionary gesture. Its narrative structure, methods of focalization and use of reported speech had much more in common with the realistic tradition of Fielding, Austen and Dickens than with the self-consciously experimental mode of Sterne. What made it different was its peculiar interface between the formal methods of classic realism and subjects and events that were patently unreal: ghosts, beings imbued with darkly supernatural powers, settings that evoked something closer to the medieval romance than the eighteenth- or nineteenth-century drawing rooms in which these novels were written and read. The most discussed female practitioner of the Gothic form is Mary Shelley, the author of *Frankenstein* (1818). Ellen Moers (1963) was the first to raise the possibility that Shelley used her tale of the horrors and murky secrecy of life creation as an analogue for her own experience of adulterous pregnancy. It would be simplistic and patronizing to assume that all women writers of the Gothic used the unreal and the supernatural as a substitute for feelings and experiences that were forbidden in public discourse. But, as we have seen, eighteenth-century prose fiction developed and refined its own stylistic and formal protocols, and in doing so it necessarily drew upon systems and discourses in which patriarchy was the norm. It could therefore be argued that women Gothic novelists achieved a degree of expressive freedom by creating an interface between a familiar, implicitly male-dominated stylistic mode and a frame of reference that was far less predictable in terms of what actually happens. Their work can best be categorized in terms of Propp's theory of narrative. The manner in which events are organized by narrative formulae is comparable with the conventions of syntax. Just as different sentences can be reduced to comparable abstract grammatical units, so the fictional modes of classic realism can be similarly reduced to interchangeable patterns. The Gothic novel borrowed its narrative syntax from the classic realist text, but altered those elements which, in Propp's scheme, would correspond with the lexical or semantic resonance of individual words. The sentence or narrative which claims that the king kidnapped the villain and demanded ransom from his own daughter is intelligible but implausible. Similarly Frankenstein's emotive and intellectual frame of reference, his ambitious and humane motives and, indeed, his implementation of them, correspond with those of other fictional characters, but his creation of a human being from a charnel house of remains disrupts the parallels between narrative and perceived reality. While Finch obtrudes an unconventional stylistic manner upon a familiar message, Shelley and other Gothic novelists combine a familiar style with a bizarre message.

It could be argued that Emily Brontë in *Wuthering Heights* has more in common with Finch than with the Gothic novelists, in that it self-consciously draws upon yet complicates the narrative formulae of classic realist fiction. The six levels of discursive exchange through which the story is mediated each strives for a degree of realism and authenticity, but their assembled complexity provides Brontë with a network of cyphers through which the sexual motives and acts of Cathy and Heathcliff become inferences and overtones.

Again we find that a woman writer is obliged to negotiate two elements of the double pattern – the literary and non-literary registers of the texts – by causing an imbalance between them. Modernism caused a far more radical imbalance and it should be noted that women writers played a significant and often pioneering role in these developments. Three women, Hilda Doolittle ('HD'), Harriet Monroe and Amy Lowell were actively involved in the Imagist rebellion against the entrapment of the lyrical 'I' within the forms and conventions of a male-dominated high culture. The following is Amy Lowell's 'Autumn':

> All day I have watched the purple vine leaves
> Fall into the water.
> And now in the moonlight they still fall,
> But each leaf is fringed with silver.

The deictic features are predominantly temporal ('All day', 'And now'). The spatial references are directed away from the addresser towards the act of perception and the image perceived. Imagism's emphasis upon external objects and linguistic transparency strips the text of the situative and stylistic registers which in traditional verse enable us to construct an impression of the addresser; and, as the riddle of the surgeon's son shows, we will often carry into this impression predetermined expectations of gender-associated roles and habits. Most significantly the poem is stripped of the gender-related conventions of metre and rhyme. While Finch is obliged to maintain an interplay between the subject of women poets and a demonstration of how she, a woman poet, can unsettle the conventions of the genre, Lowell can make use of a stylistic programme which has freed itself both from the locative associations of ordinary language and from the patriarchal inheritance of traditional form. Virginia Woolf's use of stream of consciousness as a central feature of narrative structure achieves a similar effect. According to Blain (1983: 119): 'The real bogey handed on to [Woolf] from the nineteenth century . . . was the masculine voice of the omniscient narrator.' Woolf, argues Blain, set out to 'undermine the very idea of any centralised moral stand-point, any authoritarian idea of omniscience' (ibid.: 126).

Blain's point is that the omniscient narrator commands a level of authority in the fictional text which can only be associated with the male-dominated power structures that underpin all discourses and their functions. Woolf, like Lowell, breaks the deterministic connection between literary style and the non-literary fields of power and authority that had previously informed and secured it.

Sara Mills's *Feminist Stylistics* (1995) and Deborah Cameron's *Feminism and Linguistic Theory* (1985) effectively demolish all theories of an intrinsic biological or intellectual link between style and gender, and we should by no means regard the experiments of Lowell or Woolf as indicative of a stylistic condition which best suits a woman's temperament or intellect. Ezra Pound and James Joyce were just as influential in the formation of stylistic modes which unsettled the gender associations of traditional writing.

In the following chapter, 'Evaluative Stylistics', I shall begin with two texts written by women about the relationship between men and women. Neither text is particularly experimental in form. One is explicitly biased towards traditional, patriarchal perceptions of how women behave and think; one is equally explicit in its rejection of these perceptions. The stylistic competences of both writers within their chosen forms are roughly equal. The question posed is this: is style the principal criterion for literary quality?

13

EVALUATIVE STYLISTICS

The first of the following extracts is from Barbara Cartland's novel *The Naked Battle* (1978), which I borrow from Walter Nash's *Language in Popular Fiction* (1990), whose extensive survey of 'women's' popular fiction you should compare with my own reading. The second is Fleur Adcock's poem 'Against Coupling' (1971).

> And as he kissed her, as his lips pressed themselves against her mouth, her eyes, her cheeks and the softness of her neck, Lucilla felt a fire rise within her ignited, she knew, by the fire in him.
>
> 'I love . . . you . . . ' she tried to say but her voice was deep and passionate and seemed almost to be stangled in her throat.
>
> 'You are mine!' Don Carlos cried. 'Mine completely and absolutely.'
>
> He kissed her again until she felt the world disappear and once again they were on a secret island of their own surrounded by a boundless sea.
>
> It was what she had felt when she was with him in the little Pavilion; but now it was more real, more wonderful, more intense.

Ever since she had known him she had changed and become alive to new possibilities within herself.

Now she knew she could never go back to what she was before, because she had been reborn! Reborn to a new life and above all to love.

It was a love that was perfect, and Divine, a love that was not only of the body but of the soul and the spirit.

'I love you! Oh, Carlos . . . I love you with . . . all of me!' she whispered.

He took the last words from her lips saying fiercely:

'You are mine, my beautiful, adorable wife, now and for all eternity!'

AGAINST COUPLING

I write in praise of the solitary act:
of not feeling a trespassing tongue
forced into one's mouth, one's breath
smothered, nipples crushed against the
ribcage, and that metallic tingling
in the chin set off by a certain odd nerve:

unpleasure. Just to avoid those eyes would help –
such eyes as a young girl draws life from,
listening to the vegetal
rustle within her, as his gaze
stirs polypal fronds in the obscure
sea-bed of her body, and her own eyes blur.

There is much to be said for abandoning
this no longer novel exercise –
for not 'participating in
a total experience' – when
one feels like the lady in Leeds who
had seen *The Sound of Music* eighty-six times;

or more, perhaps, like the school drama mistress
producing A Midsummer Night's Dream
for the seventh year running, with
yet another cast from 5B.
Pyramus and Thisbe are dead, but
the hole in the wall can still be troublesome.

I advise you, then, to embrace it without
encumbrance. No need to set the scene,
dress up (or undress), make speeches
Five minutes of solitude are
enough – in the bath, or to fill
that gap between the Sunday papers and lunch.

I would argue that Adcock's poem has far more claim to the status of 'good literature' than Cartland's extract, and in order to justify this argument I shall establish my working criteria.

It is possible, with a novel or a poem, to identify two textual allegiances. One is principally stylistic, in that it involves features that the text in question shares with other texts in the same genre or sub-genre: the most obvious cases of this are the narrative structure of a novel and the division of a poem into lines. The other involves formal and referential elements that are not exclusive to literature, ranging from reported speech in novels and informal syntax in free verse to topics that are just as likely to feature in conversation, philosophic treatises or on television as in literary texts. This twin allegiance has been labelled throughout the discussion so far as the double pattern.

The quality of a literary text should be judged in relation to the balance between the two dimensions of the double pattern. This scale of stylistic criteria cannot provide an objective measure of quality: our interests, tastes, types of enjoyment and values are subjective formations and will inevitably play a part in how we distinguish between good and bad writing. What the scale can provide is a comparative index, a means of identifying the particular features of literary texts which motivate our personal judgements. For example, one might pose the question, to someone with a basic knowledge of the texts: which of Joyce's three novels, *A Portrait*, *Ulysses* or *Finnegans Wake*, is his most significant contribution to literature; in short, which is the best? All manner of perspectives and criteria will influence our respondent. It could be claimed that *Finnegans Wake* is better because it is demonstrably the most experimental. Perhaps this qualifies it as the most challenging literary response to the incalculably dense, multilayered nature of twentieth-century life. It could conversely be argued that *A Portrait* and to a lesser degree *Ulysses* are better books because they maintain a level of accessibility, a narrative thread that is likely to appeal to an audience who do not have the time or inclination to ponder the relevance of formal experiments in the books they read. The criteria underpinning these two judgements are different, but both putative respondents would agree that they base them upon immutable stylistic facts: that in *Finnegans Wake* the process of mediation overwhelms and effectively obscures a clear perception of the events mediated, while in *Ulysses* and *A Portrait* there is a relative balance between form and meaning. I shall base my evaluation of Cartland and Adcock upon this perception of the double pattern. You might well disagree with my findings but you will also see that your own judgement will rely on the same tangible stylistic phenomena.

A second, more technical, consideration in literary evaluation relates to the stylistic competence of the writer. Irrespective of whether your personal affiliations lend value to this or that dimension of the double pattern, is it possible to establish how well or how badly a writer brings the two dimensions together? Is there an objective criterion for the judgement of stylistic skill? I shall address this question to a poem by William McGonagall. But first, to Cartland and Adcock.

Cartland's passage consists of two referential registers: the specific, deictic references to bodily contact and its immediate effect ('his lips pressed', 'Lucilla felt a fire', 'He kissed her again'); and linguistic terms which shift the perspective away from the immediate events to some other part of the narrative ('It was what she had felt when she was with him in the little Pavilion') or to a less specific spatio-temporal condition ('Reborn to a new life', 'now and for all eternity!', 'Mine completely and absolutely'). As the passage proceeds, the second register gradually replaces the first. The details of lips, mouth, eyes, cheek and neck and the hesitant response of the woman ('I love . . . you'), in the opening two paragraphs are specific enough, but as we read on physicality is first supplemented by simile and metaphor ('seemed almost to be strangled', 'until she felt the world disappear') and eventually replaced entirely by connotative notions of possession, spiritual unity, and submission to an overarching but unspecified condition of 'love'. The semantic and referential centre of gravity of the passage shifts towards a pattern of behavioural codes and expectations that exist independently of the novel and are inscribed within the norms of gender relations that we might refer to as utopian or conformist. Cartland's passage is in effect a self-naturalizing text. Its meaning and its signifying function are efficiently orchestrated to disclose a particular pattern of expectations.

By contrast, in Adcock's poem, there is a constant level of interference between device and meaning; between the literary features of the text and those which anchor it to a functional context. In any attempt to naturalize this text we must return again and again to the question of what exactly is 'the solitary act', praised by the speaker? The speaker, in various ways, urges us to answer, 'masturbation'. She does so by saturating the discourse with images and verbal constructions that connote the sexual act. The registers of sexual activity, and its effects and resonances, are divided in a similar way to those of Cartland's extract. We begin with the specifics ('tongue', 'mouth', 'breath', 'nipples'), move towards their less physical, more figurative, correlatives ('his gaze/stirs polypal fronds;' '"participating in a total experience"'), and on to a mildly ironic dismissal of these activities as emotive events (*The Sound of Music* and *A Midsummer Night's Dream*) transformed into hollow, ritualistic habits.

This referential pattern is supplemented by a subtle interplay of line structure and syntax that seems to generate a mood of control and submission. The major verb phrases either occur at the end of the line and cause us to push forward to a point of syntactic completion or achieve a similar effect by being cunningly (perhaps coyly) delayed until the beginning of the line ('tongue/ forced', 'without/encumbrance', for example). But when we attempt to reassemble these stylistic features as a solution to, a completion of, the text's meaning, our activity is disrupted. The text is dominated by verbal and adverbial negatives. Every elaborate reference to sexuality is qualified by a negative ('of not' 'abandoning' 'not "participating"'), until the final stanza when the reader is advised to 'embrace it'. The 'it', the 'solitary act', is it seems a total negation of all of the activities previously described. 'It' could well be masturbation; 'it' might just as plausibly be savouring one's own company, un-disturbed by the incursions of other people, sexual or non-sexual. 'It' might even refer to the process of having bipartite sex without being too involved or concerned with the efforts of the man or with the cultural-emotional associations of the act.

Adcock's text resists closure. At a localized level we can explain and specify the stylistic devices used, but their combination within the text as a whole cannot be naturalized as a single purposive discourse. Cartland encourages closure. Her stylistic strategies are a means to an end. Cartland's text displays a kind of fantastic realism, in the sense that it promotes and discloses a form of reality that is preferable to the alternatives which might be experienced by its readers.

The narrator/focalizer of Cartland's passage is as adept as those of Austen or Dickens in the management of the reader's perceptual registers: he/she is particularly good at balancing the immediate deictic features of the events described (which in real time occupy probably no more than two minutes) against a more universalized fabric of ideals, fantasies, norms and ambitions. But Cartland's focalizer employs these skills as a means of satisfying the assumed fantasies of a certain kind of reader. The stylistics of fiction are being used in a way that is comparable to the stylistics of advertising. Language organizes the perception of the reader but it does so according to an assumed notion of how the reader wants them to be organized. Adcock's realism involves a different kind of mimesis, in which the complex and often conflicting registers of the sexual act (submissive, violent, pointless, pleasurable, unpleasurable, cultural, ritualistic) are assimilated to the equally conflicting levels of verbal style within the text itself.

In purely technical terms Adcock is not a better stylist than Cartland, but, according to these criteria of value, she is a better writer. If, as in the writing of Cartland, literary style is employed exclusively to promote a particular fantasy or belief then literature itself becomes a sub-genre to all other functional and utilitarian modes of writing. Adcock, conversely, employs literary style in order to challenge the unitary, transparent relationship between language and its referent. There are, however, literary writers whose basic command of literary style raises the question of whether there are purely technical criteria which can enable us to distinguish between good and bad style.

In a 1976 article on 'Roman Jakobson's Verbal Analysis of Poetry', Paul Werth presents Jakobson's methods as the embodiment of the flaws and failed objectives of textualist stylistics. He chooses as one example a poem by William McGonagall:

> All hail to the Rev. George Gilfillan of Dundee,
> He is the greatest preacher I did ever hear or see.
> He is a man of genius bright,
> And in him his congregation does delight,

Because they find him to be honest and plain,
Affable in temper, and seldom known to complain
He preaches in a plain straightforward way,
The people flock to hear him night and day
And hundreds from the doors are often turn'd away,
Because he is the greatest preacher of the present day.
He has written the life of Sir Walter Scott,
And while he lives he will never be forgot,
Nor when he is dead,
Because by his admirers it will be often read.
And fill their minds with wonder and delight,
And wile away the tedious hours on a cold winter's night.

Werth claims, correctly, that the application to McGonagall's poem of Jakobson's exhaustive stylistic methodology would disclose levels of textual complexity comparable with those that Jakobson and Jones found in a Shakespeare sonnet. Werth's point is that Jakobson's method obscures 'a direct conflict between linguistic evidence and critical instinct', since while it discloses technical similarities between Shakespeare's and McGonagall's work it does not enable us to prove that 'the value of [McGonagall's] poem is surely abysmally low' (1976:43). This is true in the sense that Jakobson does not supplement his analyses with evaluative comments. Such an omission on Jakobson's part does not however disprove the thesis that we need to be able to analyse the stylistic features of a text objectively in order to substantiate our more subjective judgement of its quality.

McGonagall uses irregular rhythm, but so did Coleridge in 'Christabel' and so did Blake and Whitman in their most celebrated work. His rhyme scheme is unremitting but so is that of a vast number of regular poems. McGonagall's failure as a poet is due to his apparent unwillingness or inability to decide whether he is writing poetry or prose. The rhymes interfere with the progress of the syntax, but not in a way which creates a purposive tension between literary and non-literary registers. The rhymes are found and dumped at line endings as a duty to poetic convention, and syntax is altered only as a concession to this convention. If we substitute non-rhyming synonyms for the rhyme words we find a directionless, almost ungrammatical prose style:

> He preaches in a plain straightforward style, the people flock to hear him day and night, and hundreds from the doors are often turn'd away, because he is the greatest preacher of the present time.

The formal and the referential dimensions of McGonagall's verse proceed rather like two drunks walking home from the pub. Neither can entirely support the other, but they are locked together in an uncertain, undignified shuffle.

McGonagall, in his chaotic, mildly endearing way, poses a serious question for evaluative stylistics. We may judge him to be a bad poet because his failure to control and command the formal, literary dimension of language compromises his ability to absorb its referential dimension and to offer the reader an unexpected and possibly enlightening perspective on the relation between language and perceived reality. If he had written a prose essay about the activities and characteristics of the Reverend Gilfillan and told us roughly the same as he does in his poem, stylistic evaluation would be suspended. But because he uses a form in which the structural dimensions of the text constantly interfere with its communicative purpose, we begin to ask questions about how, and how well, he deals with this provocative merger of style and function. In effect naturalization becomes an evaluative rather than a purely practical procedure. McGonagall, by writing a poem, provokes our wish to naturalize the text, only to leave us disappointed. His literary style is an encumbrance, an irritation, rather than a medium which transforms or even constructs the message.

Let us now consider the role of stylistics in these evaluations of texts by Cartland, Adcock and McGonagall. Each reading has involved three levels of interpretive encounter.

Level 1: Discovery procedures

The naming of the basic operative units of a text. Stylistics, with its debt both to linguistics and to literary criticism, enables me to distinguish between those elements of a text whose main allegiance is to the network of non-literary registers and discourses – syntax and deictics in Adcock's and McGonagall's poems; reported speech and dialogue in Cartland's fiction – and those which are bound into a patently literary tradition – free verse and metre, respectively, in Adcock and McGonagall; narrational control and emphasis in Cartland: the identification of the double pattern of non-literary and literary devices.

Level 2: Naturalization

In simple terms, making sense of the text. Level 1 involves the identification of a tension between those elements which the text shares with non-literary discourses and those that are patently literary. We make sense of each text by translating it into the terms and conditions of the former: it is effectively destylized. The naturalization of Adcock's poem entails an attempt to monitor its use of literary devices to disrupt and refocus familiar registers of domestic life and sexuality. With Cartland the stylistic devices of fiction writing are deployed to promote an idealized, fantastic model of male–female relationships. McGonagall is patently incapable of properly controlling the relation between poetic and non-poetic registers. As a consequence the naturalized frame of reference (what he means) is of less significance than his stylistic incompetence.

Level 3: Judgement

The judgemental criteria proposed here are clear enough. Adcock is the best writer of the three. Her stylistic skill in the use of the double pattern is superior to McGonagall's. Cartland shares with

Adcock a degree of technical accomplishment in the management of literary and non-literary registers. However, according to these criteria, the use of this craft to challenge and unsettle familiar perceptions of reality (Adcock) is regarded as superior to its use to project, maybe satisfy, an idealized, fantastic idea of how people should behave (Cartland).

It is not my intention to offer my criteria for good literature as official and conclusive: they are mine and they are probably symptomatic of my various sociocultural affiliations. More significant is my use of the three levels of interpretive encounter; the first two incorporating the disciplines of stylistics, the third relating these to a specific system of aesthetic, perhaps ideological, values.

We need to be reasonably competent in the first two to confidently articulate our experience of the third, which involves everything from the specialized polemic of academic criticism, through book reviewing to personal taste and reading habits.

In an influential essay called 'How to Recognise a Poem When You See One' (1980) Stanley Fish describes how, when teaching a course on the religious lyric, he asked his class to interpret a modern lyric chalked on the classroom blackboard. This 'text' is actually a list of surnames left over from the previous class on linguistics (to add a sardonic edge the names are those of major US literary-linguists of the 1960s and 1970s):

> Jacobs – Rosenbaum
> Levin
> Thorne
> Hayes
> Ohman (?)

His students demonstrated an apparent competence in levels 1 and 2.

> The first line of the poem (the very order of events assumed the already constituted status of the object) received the most attention:

Jacobs was explicated as a reference to Jacob's ladder, traditionally allegorized as a figure for the Christian ascent to heaven. In this poem, however, or so my students told me, the means of ascent is not a ladder but a tree, a rose tree or rosenbaum. This was seen as an obvious reference to the Virgin Mary who was often characterised as a rose without thorns, itself an emblem of the immaculate conception.

(1980: 324)

Fish's description of their analysis continues for a further 500 words. This experiment, which Fish claims to have performed with similar results in '9 or 10 universities in 3 countries', supports his claim that 'acts of recognition, rather than being triggered by formal characteristics, are their source' (ibid.: 326).

What Fish calls the 'act of recognition', identifying the text as a poem, occurs in my model at level 1: two patterns are recognized, one which the poem will share with all other language forms (syntax, lexis, semantics) and one which is unique to poetic writing (line divisions). Fish's students seem to have done this, in that it was the line divisions of the text which provided the framework for their tracing of religious references (in my model, level 2).

Fish's thesis that the formal structures of literary texts are a function of interpretive strategies would have collapsed had he or his students moved on to level 3, the point at which we address the questions of why, to what effect and how well the author employs the formal structures of a text. They might have asked what this alleged poet had hoped to achieve by leaving out verb phrases. Their literary competence might have prompted a comparison with Imagist verse or with Williams's 'Spring and All' in which syntactic continuities are cut down to a bare minimum. They might then have noted that while much of Williams's or Imagist verse challenges the regularities of syntax and line structure it does so by making use of them – not by leaving them out. Finally they might have considered how a reader could enjoy, admire, be puzzled or stimulated by a poem, when that reader has to supply the verb phrases and patterns of coherence that turn it into something that is recognizable as a poem. Moreover, some readers might claim that the blackboard poet's complete abandonment of form, syntax and coherence is, for them, invigorating. But to do so they would have to acknowledge that it causes them to feel this way because of its demonstrable, intrinsic difference from poems that involve form, syntax and coherence, not because their interpretive strategies have made it different from other poems.

It is clear from this that there is a necessary mutual dependence between what Fish calls 'acts of recognition', the objective specification of formal characteristics (levels 1 and 2), and the more subjective experience of how we think or feel about these characteristics. The latter cannot properly be addressed without some reference to the former: our enjoyment or dislike of a text must be caused by something in it. Fish therefore presents a challenge to stylistics. He questions the fundamental assumption upon which stylistics is based: that we can specify generic categories – literary, non-literary; poetic, non-poetic – by our identification of intrinsic textual features.

Terry Eagleton, in *Literary Theory: An Introduction* (1983) continues the assault. Eagleton regards stylistics, and its function in the broader educational and cultural consensus of evaluation and taste, as part of an ideological conspiracy. His argument runs as follows. The objective of distinguishing between literary and non-literary features of texts (promoted by the Formalists and sponsored by the New Critics) leads to a dangerously apolitical brand of literary criticism. The Formalist notion of literary style as non-pragmatic, self-referential language causes us to detach the literary text from the pragmatic real world of political and social issues. Such head-in-the-sand aesthetics prevents us from recognizing that what we might value as good literature is effectively a construct of the ideological prejudices and preconditions of a particular society or period:

Literature, in the sense of a set of works or assured and unalterable values, distinguished by certain shared inherent properties, does not exist.

(1983: 11)

If Eagleton is correct in this, then the book you are now reading is self-deluding fiction. A final test case is called for which will address Eagleton's two principal contentions: (1) that the distinction between literary and non-literary registers (the notion of the double pattern) is an interpretive fiction; (2) that a belief in literature as 'different' blinds us to its sociopolitical resonances.

Eagleton gives an example of how an imposed literary reading would prevent us from appreciating the political and social significance of Orwell's essays on the Spanish Civil War, because as literary readers we would function 'as though the topics [Orwell] discussed were less important than the way he discussed them' (1983: 8). Orwell's essays present an intriguing problem because he frequently unsettles the borderlines between factual journalism and fiction. Often the narrator will be identifiable as George Orwell (or Eric Blair) only by the name beneath the title. Within the text the narrational presence will defer, anonymously, to the stylistic character of the account in a way that recalls Chatman's notion of the 'implied author' in fiction (above, p. 55). A well-known example of this occurs in a story-report by Orwell called 'A Hanging' (1931).

David Lodge in a 1977 discussion of this text covers much the same ground as Eagleton and, with regard to the question of whether 'A Hanging' is literary or non-literary, he concludes that

the answer probably depends upon the context in which it is read, and the expectations of the individual reader. It is not foregrounded as literature in any obvious way – indeed it could be said to disguise itself as non literature . . . though there are certain significant

> absences in the text which perhaps operate as signs of literariness at an almost subliminal level, and covertly invite literary reading.
>
> (1977: 17)

In short, yes and no. We can agree with some aspects of Lodge's second sentence, but he grossly understates his case. In fact, 'A Hanging' displays a tension between Shklovsky's notions of *fabula* (the narrative and its subject) and *sjuzet* (the technique of narration) that would stand comparison with Shklovsky's favourite, *Tristram Shandy*.

The real-time sequence of the events narrated effectively governs the narrative structure of the text. Each paragraph is anchored to a particular event in a sequence from when the police and officials meet, escort the condemned man from his cell, cross the prison yard to the gallows, hang him and return for a drink, a smoke and a chat. The first-person narrator is almost obsessively concerned with detail. He tells us of the exact colour of hair, type of clothing, posture, height and weight of the participants. He cautiously transcribes dialogue which reveals the stress patterns, accents, pronunciation and locutionary habits of middle-class, military English and at least two registers of Burmese English. He tells us of the number of planks on the scaffold, the colour and texture of buildings, weeds and gravel, and specifies, in yards, his position in relation to other participants and the distance between the cells and the gallows. He maintains an emphasis on what is observable to him within the spatio-temporal boundaries of the event.

This foregrounding of the components of the *fabula* causes a number of tensions with the *sjuzet*. The narrative is retrospective, in the past tense, and the question of how someone writing later can recollect so much, and make such detail conform to a narrative structure, prompts comparison, as we saw earlier, with the equally strange collision of pragmatic and non-pragmatic timescales in Fielding's *Moll Flanders*. The only point at which the narrator shifts the focalizing angle from documentary detail to personal reflection is in the middle of the text (the tenth paragraph of twenty-four), a shift prompted by the prisoner's avoidance of a puddle on the path. The following is approximately one-third of this reflective paragraph:

> His nails would still be growing when he stood on the drop, when he was falling through the air with a tenth of a second to live. His eyes saw the yellow gravel and the grey walls, and his brain still remembered, foresaw, reasoned – reasoned even about puddles. He and we were a party of men, walking together, seeing, hearing, feeling, understanding the same world; and in two minutes, with a sudden snap, one of us would be gone – one mind less, one world less.

The narrator, like Shandy, has stopped a sequence which elsewhere seems to be propelled entirely by external events, and the more we read the text the more we become aware of the paradoxical relation between the event-driven narrative and the degree of control exercised by the narrator.

If we were to leave out paragraph 10 we could easily switch the tense of the rest of the text from past to present without altering anything but the verbs. But at the same time this would strengthen its fictional, literary register. It is even less plausible for a hanging to be described in such a composed, syntactically organized manner at the time that it happens than it is for the narrator to have recollected so much detail after the event. In any case, such an alteration would be impossible without the removal of paragraph 10. Paragraph 10 foregrounds the retrospective, fictive control of the narrator yet contrasts sharply and somewhat implausibly with the perceptual immediacy of the rest of the text. Orwell, by causing these tensions, seems to have prised the text out of the pragmatic field in which we judge language in relation to the events that it purports to describe: it qualifies as fiction.

The interesting question is: why does Orwell do this? We know from personal and biographical accounts that Orwell attended a hanging in Burma and we know also that he shares the narrator's moral and physical revulsion for capital punishment. If the apparent purpose of the text is to arouse in the reader the same feelings of shame and disgust at a regular feature of British and colonial life, why does he fictionalize it?

The answer is that its literary structure has a far more compelling and disturbing effect on the reader than would result from a self-evidently journalistic account. What Lodge describes as a subliminal and covert literary 'reading' is actually a carefully planned textual effect. The almost surreal collision of reality and unreality felt by the narrator as the prisoner avoids the puddle is in a broader sense communicated to the reader by the text's shifts between functional and non-functional registers. The disruption of the stylistic fabric of the text in paragraph 10 is caused apparently by an event outside the text. (The shift is comparable with the blank verse/prose alternations of Lucio's and Claudio's dialogue in *Measure for Measure*, see above, pp. 120–1). The referential context survives the shift in stylistic register, but our perceptions of it are radically altered. The effect of this on the reader of 'A Hanging' is mimetic in that it corresponds with the narrator's sudden realization that the indifferent sequence of events he describes involves the destruction of, as he puts it, another 'world'.

Eagleton claims that when reading a Robert Burns poem 'as literature' we are not supposed to enquire about the potentially real events that underpin the self-referring fabric of the words (p. 8). Orwell demonstrates that it is possible to create a text which satisfies all of the Formalist criteria for literariness but which also obliges us to go through the words and to examine the relationship between what the words do and what they seek to represent. It is, judged against the three-level scheme, excellent literature. The narrator controls the relation between the functional and non-functional registers with seamless authority. He allows the *fabula*, the event-driven discourse, to absorb the reader's interpretive faculties for approximately 1,500 words so that the shift in focalization is all the more surprising and effective. More significantly, he at once alters yet secures the boundaries between literary and non-literary texts. Stylistically 'The Hanging' qualifies as a short story and there is no evidence to prompt us to read it as journalism. It is by Eric Blair but the text presents us with no locative political or personal connection between Blair and the narrator: only the reader who knows something of the life of Blair/Orwell can make this connection. It also gathers into its textual, stylistic field a whole network of pragmatic registers, sociopolitical issues and judicial facts that constitute the real world of the writer and reader of the *Adelphi* magazine in 1931. It takes on a patently non-pragmatic stylistic structure in order to foreground more starkly events and issues that we would expect to be addressed in pragmatic discourse. In purely stylistic terms (levels 1 and 2) it is comparable with Cartland; but with regard to its use of the double pattern to oblige us to confront rather than avoid reality (levels 1 and 3) it is superior.

Contra Eagleton, it may be argued that reading 'A Hanging' as literature – using the analytical tools of stylistics – enables us to foreground its moral and political message. Our appreciation of its literary quality does not marginalize its non-literary message; rather it shows us how clearly and effectively this message is conveyed.

BIBLIOGRAPHY

Aristotle. *The Works of Aristotle translated into English*, ed. W.D. Ross, Oxford: Oxford University Press (1924).

Auerbach, Erich. *Mimesis*, New York: Doubleday (1957; first pub. 1946).

Austin, J.L. *How To Do Things With Words*, Oxford: Oxford University Press (1962).

Bakhtin, Mikhail. *Voprosy literatury i éstetiki*, in *The Dialogic Imagination*, Austin, Texas: University of Texas Press (1981; first pub. 1934–5).

—— 'From The Prehistory of Novelistic Discourse' (1967; reprinted in Lodge, 1988).

Barthes, Roland. *Elements of Semiology*, London: Cape (1967; first pub. 1964).

—— *Système de la Mode*, Paris: Seuil (1967).

—— *Writing Degree Zero*, New York: Hill and Wang (1968; first pub. 1952).

—— *S/Z*, London: Cape (1975; first pub. 1970).

Beardsley, M. and Wimsatt, W. K. 'The International Fallacy' (1947) in Wimsatt (1954).

Belsey, Catherine. *Critical Practice*, London: Methuen (1980).

Bersani, Leo. *A Future for Astyanax: Character and Desire in Literature*, London: Marion Boyars (1978).

Blain, V. 'Narrative Voice and the Female Perspective in Virginia Woolf's Early Novels', in *Virginia Woolf: New Critical Essays*, ed. P. Clements and I. Grundy, London: Vision Press (1983).

Booth, Wayne. *The Rhetoric of Fiction*, Chicago: Chicago University Press (1961).

Bradford, Richard. *A Linguistic History of English Poetry*, London: Routledge (1993).

—— *Roman Jakobson. Life, Language, Art*, London: Routledge (1994).

Brogan, T.V.F. (ed.) *English Versification, 1570–1980. A Reference Guide with Global Appendix*, Baltimore: Johns Hopkins University Press (1981).

Brooks, Cleanth. *The Well Wrought Urn. Studies in the Structure of Poetry*, London: Methuen (1968; first pub. 1947).

Brooks, Cleanth and Warren, Robert Penn. *Understanding Poetry*, New York: Holt, Rinehart and Winston (1938; 3rd edn 1960).

Brown, Laura. *Alexander Pope*, Oxford: Basil Blackwell (1985).

Cameron, Deborah. *Feminism and Linguistic Theory*, London: Macmillan (1985).

Caudwell, Christopher. *Illusion and Reality. A Study of the Sources of Poetry*, London: Lawrence and Wishart (1946).

Chatman, Seymour. 'Robert Frost's "Mowing": An Inquiry into Prosodic Structure', *Kenyon Review* 18 (1956), 421–38.

—— *Story and Discourse*, Ithaca, NY: Cornell University Press (1978).

Chomsky, Noam. *Syntactic Structures*, The Hague: Mouton (1957).

—— *Aspects of the Theory of Syntax*, Cambridge, MA: MIT Press (1965).

Cixous, Hélène. 'The Laugh of the Medusa', in *New French Feminisms: An Anthology*, ed. E. Marks and I. de Courtivron, Brighton: Harvester (1981).

Culler, Jonathan. *Structuralist Poetics. Structuralism, Linguistics and the Study of Literature*, London: Routledge (1975).

Davie, Donald. *Articulate Energy: An Inquiry into the Syntax of English Poetry*, London: Routledge (1955).

Eagleton, Mary (ed.) *Feminist Literary Theory. A Reader*, Oxford: Basil Blackwell (1986).

Eagleton, Terry. *Literary Theory: An Introduction*, Oxford: Basil Blackwell (1983).

Easthope, Antony. *Poetry as Discourse*, London: Methuen (1983).

Empson, William. *Seven Types of Ambiguity*, Harmondsworth: Penguin (1961; first pub. 1930).

Fish, Stanley. *Is There a Text in this Class? The Authority of Interpretive Communities*, Cambridge, MA: Harvard University Press (1980).

—— 'How to Recognise a Poem When You See One', in *Is There a Text in This Class?* (1980).

Foucault, Michel. *The Order of Things*, London: Tavistock (1970).

Fowler, Roger. *Linguistics and the Novel*, London: Methuen (1977).

—— *Literature as Social Discourse*, London: Batsford (1981).

Genette, Gérard. *Narrative Discourse*, Ithaca, NY: Cornell University Press (1980; first pub. 1972).

Gilbert, S. 'Patriarchal Poetry and Women Readers: Reflections on Milton's Bogey', *PMLA* 93 (1978), 368–82.

Gilbert, S. and Gubar, S. *The Madwoman in the Attic: The Woman Writer and the Nineteenth Century Imagination*, New Haven, CT: Yale University Press (1979).

Greimas, A.J. *Sémantique structurale*, Paris: Larousse (1966).

—— *Du Sens*, Paris: Seuil (1970).

Halliday, M.A.K. *Language as Social Semiotic*, London: Edward Arnold (1978).

Halliday, M.A.K. and Hasan, R. *Cohesion in English*, London: Longman (1976).

Hobsbaum, Philip. *Metre, Rhythm and Verse Form*, London: Routledge (1996).

Hollander, John. *Vision and Resonance: Two Senses of Poetic Form*, Oxford: Oxford University Press (1975).

Jacobus, Mary. 'The Difference of View', in *Women Writing about Women*, ed. M. Jacobus, London: Croom Helm (1979).

Jakobson, Roman. 'Closing Statement: Linguistics and Poetics', in *Style in Language*, ed. T. Sebeok, Cambridge, MA: MIT Press (1960). References from reprint in Lodge (1988).

—— *Selected Writings, I*, The Hague: Mouton (1971).

—— *Selected Writings. III*, The Hague: Mouton (1980).

—— *Language in Literature*, ed. K. Pomorska and S. Rudy, Cambridge, MA: Harvard University Press (1987).

Jakobson, Roman and Halle, Morris. *Fundamentals of Language*, The Hague: Mouton (1956).

Kristeva, Julia. *Semiotikè: recherches pour une sémanalyse*, Paris: Seuil (1969).

Leech, G.N. *A Linguistic Guide to English Poetry*, London: Longman (1969).

Leech, G.N. and Short, M. *Style in Fiction*, London: Longman (1981).

Levin, Samuel. *Linguistic Structures in Poetry*, The Hague: Mouton (1962).

—— 'The Conventions of Poetry', in *Literary Style. A Symposium*, ed. Seymour Chatman, London: Oxford University Press (1971).

Lodge, David (ed.) *Twentieth Century Literary Criticism. A Reader*, London: Longman (1972).

—— *The Modes of Modern Writing. Metaphor, Metonymy, and the Typology of Modern Literature*, London: Edward Arnold (1977).

—— '*Middlemarch* and the Idea of the Classic Realist Text', in *The Nineteenth Century Novel: Critical Essays and Documents*, ed. A. Kettle, London: Heinemann (1981).

—— (ed.) *Modern Criticism and Theory. A Reader*, London: Longman (1988).

MacCabe, Colin. *James Joyce and the Revolution of the Word*, London: Macmillan (1978).

McHale, B. 'Free Indirect Discourse: a Survey of Recent Accounts', *Poetics and Theory of Literature* 3 (1978), 235–87.

McLain, R. 'Literary Criticism versus Generative Grammars', *Style* 10 (1976), 231–53.

Mayo, Robert. 'The Contemporaneity of the *Lyrical Ballads*', *PMLA* 69 (1954), 486–522.

Mills, Sara. *Feminist Stylistics*, London: Routledge (1995).

Moers, Ellen. *Literary Women*, London: W.H. Allen (1963).

Nash, Walter. *Language in Popular Fiction*, London: Routledge (1990).

Ohmann, Richard. 'Generative Grammars and the Concept of Literary Style', in *Linguistics and Literary Style*, New York: Holt and Rinehart (1970; first pub. 1964).

—— 'Speech Acts and the Definition of Literature', *Philosophy and Rhetoric* 4 (1971), 1–19.

Pascal, R. *The Dual Voice: Free Indirect Speech and its Functioning in the Nineteenth Century Novel*, Manchester: Manchester University Press (1977).

Perry, Menakhem. 'Literary Dynamics: How the Order of a Text Creates Meanings', *Poetics Today* 1 (1979), 35–64.

Plato. *The Collected Dialogues*, ed. E. Hamilton and H. Cairns, New York (1963).

—— *The Republic*, trans. B. Jowett, Oxford: Clarendon Press (1888).

Propp, Vladimir. *The Morphology of the Folktale*, Austin: University of Texas Press (1968; first pub. 1928).

Puttenham, George. *The Arte of English Poesie* (1589). Reprinted in *Elizabethan Critical Essays*, ed. G. Gregory Smith, Oxford: Oxford University Press (1904).

Ransom, John Crowe. 'Criticism Inc.' (1937) in Lodge (1972).

Richards, I.A. *The Philosophy of Rhetoric*, London: Oxford University Press (1936).

Riffaterre, Michael. 'Describing Poetic Structures: Two Approaches to Baudelaire's "Les Chats"', *Yale French Studies* 36, 7 (1966), 200–42.

Rimmon-Kenan, S. *Narrative Fiction: Contemporary Poetics*, London: Methuen (1983).

Shklovsky, Viktor. 'Art as Technique' (1917), in *Russian Formalist Criticism. Four Essays*, ed. L. Lemon and M. Reis, Lincoln: University of Nebraska Press (1965).

—— 'Sterne's *Tristram Shandy*: Stylistic Commentary' (1921), in Lemon and Reis (1965).

Thorne, J.P. 'Stylistics and Generative Grammars', *Journal of Linguistics* 1 (1965), 49–59.

Todorov, T. *Grammaire du Decameron*, The Hague: Mouton (1969).

Werth, Paul. 'Roman Jakobson's Verbal Analysis of Poetry', *Journal of Linguistics* 12 (1976), 21–73.

Wimsatt, W.K. *The Verbal Icon*, Lexington: University of Kentucky Press (1954).

INDEX